FORGOTTEN SAINT:

THE LIFE OF THEODORE FRELINGHUYSEN

A Case Study of Christian Leadership

By

Robert J. Eells

UNIVERSITY
PRESS OF
AMERICA

Lanham • New York • London

Trinity
Christian
College

Copyright © 1987 by

University Press of America,® Inc.

4720 Boston Way
Lanham, MD 20706

3 Henrietta Street
London WC2E 8LU England

Printed in the United States of America

British Cataloging in Publication Information Available

Co-published by arrangement with Trinity Christian College

ISBN: 0-8191-6606-5 (pbk. : alk. paper)
ISBN: 0-8191-6605-7 (alk. paper)

All University Press of America books are produced on acid-free
paper which exceeds the minimum standards set by the National
Historical Publication and Records Commission.

For Janice

Acknowledgments

A project such as this one requires the support of many people. Emotional support and encouragement as well as helpful comments came from my colleague in Trinity Christian's history department, Dr. Robert Rice. Dr. Burton Rozema, our Academic Dean, also gave his support as well as the "freedom" to write despite my heavy teaching load.

Research would have been difficult, if not impossible, without the aid of a good research librarian. Jean Strong proved to be my savior in this area, especially through her tireless efforts involving the inter-library loan system.

Bonnie Decker, our faculty secretary and typist, somehow found the time to complete this manuscript. And she was more than a "mere" typist, serving also as my first editor and initial critic. She made my job much easier.

The principal editing job fell to another colleague, Dr. Dan Diephouse, of the English department. I am deeply in his debt for the time and effort he gave to smoothing out my style and making the final rough draft readable. I can hardly imagine a more gracious and helpful partner.

Some of the final research and initial writing took place in the summer of 1985 at Brandeis University in Waltham, Massachusetts. I was at Brandeis for a summer seminar sponsored by the National Endowment for the Humanities. I am grateful to the NEH for its support.

Table of Contents

		Page
Preface		ix
Introduction		xiii
Chapter 1	Gracious Living	1
Chapter 2	New Jersey's Rising Star	7
Chapter 3	Here I Stand	15
Chapter 4	Statesmanship and "Friendly Persuasion"	29
Chapter 5	5,106	37
Chapter 6	A Whig America, A Christian America?	47
Chapter 7	Colonization: A Case of Missing the Boat?	59
Chapter 8	Benevolent Emperor	71
Chapter 9	Nurturing Father	81
Chapter 10	Full-time Evangelist	93
Chapter 11	Heart, Home, and Sanctuary	103
Chapter 12	Leadership	115
Bibliography		127
Index		133

Preface

Bad government is more terrible than tigers.

—Confucius

Chicago is a truly great American city—full of life and energy, restless, changing, the epitome of urban existence in America. It was thus with "great expectations" that my wife, Janice, and I moved to Chicago in 1982. We wanted to be a part of this dynamic metropolitan experiment, and in some small ways we hoped to shape our environment, shape it as evangelical Christians committed to a God who cares for people and cities.

Chicago has met many of our expectations and been the recipient of a few of our modest efforts at Christian service. But one disappointment remains: the experience—mostly vicarious—of "Chicago style" politics. Oh, we had heard many rumors about Chicago politics and politicians, the usual stories of corruption and chicanery, of authoritarian city bosses and voters who continue to cast ballots from the grave! But nothing really prepared us for the shock of exposure to what passes as political leadership and discourse in this "vanguard" city. Since the election of Mayor Harold Washington in 1983, the situation has gone from bad to worse, from the semi-feudal paternalism of Boss Daley to the semi-barbarian warfare of the mayor and the city council.

We used to joke about this chaos with our friends, even our Christian friends. It was always good for a few laughs as relationships unfolded. But it's not funny anymore, only sad—and embarrassing. Our Christian friends mourn, as do many others.

My vocation is college teaching, history and political science. I have spent many hours over the last three years trying to understand Chicago politics in the context of Biblical norms and western history. This effort has given me the perspective to see that one missing ingredient in Chicago politics, and American politics and society in general, is *leadership*. Putting it bluntly and using Biblical language, our "leaders," those political and cultural figures with power, usually lack the gift of leadership: they lack the ability to exercise an office of authority with wisdom and compassion. And power exercised without insight and mercy leads to brokenness. The truth of this observation can be seen all too clearly in recent Chicago history.

Absence of such a gift among secular politicians and other cultural figures is not surprising. It's what we should expect, a "normal" occurrence. When this gift appears, when traits of true leadership become manifest, it's an exception to the rule. Fortunately, exceptions have occurred in our history. We have been blessed occasionally by individuals who possessed some genuine leadership qualities. In the political realm such names come to mind as George Washington, Thomas Jefferson, Henry Clay, Abraham Lincoln, Teddy and Franklin D. Roosevelt. Additional names could be found representing other important areas of American life, such as education, labor, and the military. We should be thankful for these individuals and for the leadership they have provided.

As evangelicals, however, I think our primary concern should be the history of Christian leadership, of leadership models founded upon Biblical insight and personal commitment to Christ—as Lord as well as Savior. Here, too, leadership has been evident, but not to the extent expected, at least not up to my expectations. William Jennings Bryan is an example from the turn of the century of an evangelical politician whose impact was profound; Jimmy Carter is another more contemporary model. Others could be mentioned, but not as many as would be expected in light of our nearly two hundred years' experience as evangelicals in America. Further, when we look for evangelicals who have demonstrated leadership in several "public" areas at the same time, or over a lifetime, the search is even less rewarding. Evangelical America has produced few "Renaissance men" in the public arena, that is, men or women who have made significant contributions to a range of issues and institutions which lay outside of the general framework of the church.

I believe that I have found one such versatile leader, namely, Theodore Frelinghuysen of New Jersey (1787-1862). The context of my discovery is interesting, perhaps fitting. At the outset, I had only a dim memory of a pre-Civil War Christian leader whose name was the same as a notable revivalist of the First Great Awakening, Theodore J. Frelinghuysen. My renewed contact came through research involving William Wilberforce, the English abolitionist and Christian politician. Somewhat frustrated in searching for well-rounded public leadership by Christians in America, I had turned to nineteenth-century England. Here, I naturally concentrated on Wilberforce as the best exmple of a truly public Christian life. Politics, missions, education, voluntary associations of all kinds—little seemed to be outside of his field of interest or active endeavor. At one point in my research I discovered a passing reference to Frelinghuysen as an "American Wilberforce," an evangelical Christian actively involved in social and political issues. What an encouraging discovery! The rest is history, as they say.

I intend this book to be a brief "case study" of Christian leadership. I recognize that leadership is a complex phenomenon and that it is only one dimension of the overall problem of Christian involvement in the world. But it is surely a crucial one, nonetheless. If we need anything today as evangelicals, we need strong, principled, loving leadership, not only for our community but for the nation at large. Without it our situation becomes unfocused, without direction. With it we can enjoy some of the shalom that comes as a reward for godly living.

My approach, then, will be to use the life of Theodore Frelinghuysen as a model for the case study approach. I am not writing to increase the reader's historical knowledge, *per se*, although evangelicals certainly need to become better acquainted with their own family tree. My primary purpose, rather, is to encourage evangelicals to consider public service as a calling that is just as important as the choice to become a pastor, elder, or church musician. Theodore Frelinghuysen's life is a shining example of the power of the gospel to illuminate the many paths of service which God has already laid out before us. I'm excited about his life, and I've learned much from it. My prayer is that some of this excitement will be sensed and appropriated by the reader, too.

In order to focus attention through Frelinghuysen's life onto our contemporary world, I have included a section of questions at the conclusion of each chapter. My intention is to guide the reader to some of the possible lessons to be learned from the life of this departed Christian leader. I hope that college or adult education classes will use these questions as a springboard for further discussion. Accept, reject, revise; in a word—enjoy.

Introduction

It may fairly be said perhaps that he was the leading layman
of the country in Christian movements of his day.
        —William Demarest on Frelinghuysen, 1924

Andrew Jackson was no lover of Indians. In fact, he owed his presidency in part to his reputation as an Indian fighter. For this macho frontiersman the only good Indian was a dead Indian—or at least one who would pack up and leave when white settlers felt the need for more space. During his first term (1829-1833), he made it clear that the Cherokee Indians of Georgia would have to leave, to abandon their homes and flee to the West. He sided with Georgia's claim of sovereignty, even thumbing his nose against the U. S. Supreme Court's decision (1831) in favor of the legal and constitutional rights of the Cherokee tribe. "John Marshall has made his decision; now let him enforce it," declared the president sarcastically. Not many politicians had the courage to oppose the popular Jackson when his mind was made up.

One man did—Theodore Frelinghuysen. On April 6, 1830, Frelinghuysen rose in the Senate to defend the Cherokees. No one would have blamed him for having a dry mouth and a rapid heartbeat. This was virtually a "maiden" speech for the freshman senator. And it had to be delivered before colleagues of the stature of Robert Hayne, Daniel Webster, Thomas Hart Benton, and Vice-President John Calhoun! Frelinghuysen cleared his throat and began speaking. When he finished six hours later, he had delivered what scholars consider to be a classic in senatorial eloquence and persuasiveness. His contemporaries were also impressed. Because of this speech and others on a variety of subjects (like the sanctity of the Sabbath), he quickly came to be regarded as the leading "Christian statesman" of his day. Evangelicals were delighted to see such a leader emerge in the political arena, although newspaper articles and editorials sometimes used this label—"Christian statesman"—derisively. Frelinghuysen was not disturbed; the English press had also mocked his hero, Wilberforce, in much the same way. He wore the label proudly, not being ashamed to carry the name "Christian" wherever he traveled, wherever the Spirit and Word of God led him.

The extent of his ministry is truly impressive. In 1817 he was appointed by the New Jersey legislature as attorney general, a post he held for twelve years. As attorney general, and later as a private attorney, he was involved in almost all of the important court cases argued in the New Jersey state system. His job as attorney general was so challenging that he even turned down an appointment to the state Supreme Court in 1826. In 1829 he was appointed by the legislature as U. S. senator, serving with distinction until 1835. During his years in the Senate, he struggled as a Christian with the momentous issues of the age: slavery, tariff reform, currency regulation (the Bank of the United States), veterans' benefits, federalism (the power of the executive), as well as the Indian rights controversy. Newark, New Jersey, elected him as mayor in 1837 and 1838, an important office because of the financial distress suffered by urban communities in the wake of the Panic of 1837. Finally, his political career crested in 1844 when he was nominated by the Whig party to run for vice-president beside the venerable Henry Clay. This nomination was no fluke. It appears that Frelinghuysen was chosen precisely because his Christian character was spotless and his Christian convictions were well known.

Politics, however, was only one of the many arenas in which public Christian leadership could be exercised in antebellum America. In the Age of Jackson "public" and "private" were not so easily distinguished. Wherever social reform was being attempted, public service was being rendered, and true leadership was being displayed. It was in this larger sense that Frelinghuysen's star really sparkled.

In antebellum America "benevolent societies" were in the vanguard of efforts at social improvement. These organizations had as their goal the moral reformation of America. And Frelinghuysen was the undisputed champion of these institutions. According to Clifford S. Griffin, Frelinghuysen was "the greatest hero that benevolent societies ever had." An impressive list of organizations drew upon his talents: the American Board of Commissioners for Foreign Missions, the American Bible Society, the American Tract Society, the American Sunday School Union, the Congressional Temperance Society, and the American Colonization Society. Frelinghuysen helped supervise these societies as they launched efforts to realize as much of the Kingdom of God on earth as is humanly possible.

Commitment to moral reformation also drove Frelinghuysen to dedicate the last portion of his life to education. He believed that if America was to be a truly righteous nation, her youth had to be properly trained—at all levels, but especially in higher education. The strength of this commitment drew him away from the legal profession and politics, a remarkable sacrifice for such a political being. He thus spent the last twenty-three years of his life providing leadership in education as chancellor of New York University and president of Rutgers College.

Finally, the church should not be overlooked. Although my study will concentrate on nonchurch organizations, Frelinghuysen's church leadership will be noted, for he was a strong supporter of the church as institution and organism. He realized, correctly, that active involvement with the world must be built upon the solid foundation of both personal piety and the organized fellowship of believers.

In light of these accomplishments, why has Theodore Frelinghuysen been largely ignored by scholars and evangelicals? The answer, I think, for scholars—secular scholars—is obvious: they have little interest in "Christian statesmanship." For them, Frelinghuysen was a thinly disguised theocrat, a threat to the evolution of egalitarian democracy in America. This attitude is typically expressed by Arthur Schlesinger, Jr., in his massive study, *The Age of Jackson.* Schlesinger can barely contain his contempt for Frelinghuysen, dismissing him as a "staunch conservative," a man of "persevering religiosity," a man who did not recognize that the wave of the future in America was a secular one. Schlesinger's approach has been the dominant one among mainstream historians.

The situation among evangelicals, however, is a different story. A lack of historical interest and knowledge is part of the answer, at least for the general community. But what of evangelical scholars? Why have they overlooked Frelinghuysen? (Why did I have so little awareness of him?) Three reasons stand out: First, evangelical historians and social scientists are trained at secular universities where a man like Frelinghuysen elicits little sympathy. Second, much of the fine historical scholarship appearing lately from evangelicals focuses upon individuals and churches from the non-Reformed tradition, from Wesleyan, Holiness, and Pentecostal sources, Don Dayton's *Discovering an Evangelical Heritage* and Timothy Smith's *Revivalism and Social Reform,* for example. Since Frelinghuysen represented the Presbyterian and Reformed community, he is set aside by definition. Third, much of his leadership was of a pietistic nature, involving a lifetime of personal, private relationships with people from all walks of life. In this sense it's easy to understand how Frelinghuysen would be passed over. Most of the evidence comes from letters, diaries, and recollections not available to the general reader, or even the scholar—unless he knows what to look for and where to look. Part of the burden of this study will be to examine the "personal side" of Frelinghuysen's spiritual leadership.

Another reason for seeing Frelinghuysen as a possible model for leadership is the fundamental similarity between the issues facing him and those confronting evangelicals in today's world. By "fundamental" I do not mean "identical" but "structurally similar." What burdened him also disturbs us, although in altered form: slavery has been abolished, but who would argue that racism died with it; tariff reform looks like a dead issue until we probe a little deeper into the debate over balance of payments and skyrocketing budget deficits; "currency reform" continues to make headlines in response to the galloping inflation of the late 1970's and in light of the political independence of the Federal Reserve Board; veterans' benefits are once again a hot item in post-Vietnam America; federalism has returned to center stage, thanks to Nixon and Reagan; and the rights of Indians and other ethnic minorities continue to be a matter of concern in the wake of the civil rights crusade of the 1960's.

Looking at Frelinghuysen's life and witness won't solve all our problems, by any means. But it will give us a fresh start and new insight.

Chapter 1

Gracious Legacy

[Theordore's grandmother] was a woman or remarkable pei-
ty. Her life was spent in prayer, reading the Word of God,
and commending religion to the notice and regard of all. No
one came near her without hearing a good word spoken in
favor of the Lord Jesus Christ and His service.
—William Campbell on Dinah Hardenberg, 1862

The year was 1800. Young Theodore was determined; he had made
up his mind; there was no changing it. He would leave school and become a farmer. He had discussed the topic with his father, Frederick,
who seemed open to the prospect. Now all he had to do was convince
his stepmother, Ann. (His mother, Gertrude, had died in 1794.) Theodore approached her cautiously, realizing that she would not be as pli-
ant as his father. His stepmother had always encouraged him in his
studies, supervising his progress, helping choose for him (and his younger
brother, Frederick) a proper grammar school in 1798. She would not
be easily convinced. But try he must, for he was thirteen years old and
weary of school! Two years of additional study at the grammar school
in New Brunswick had been more than enough for him.

The young rebel was right to be worried about his stepmother's reaction. Although she listened patiently to his plea and did not immediately challenge him, it was obvious that she was not pleased with his
decision. There would be no dropping out of school for Theodore, she
quietly resolved. Being a farmer was fine for others, but her stepson
required more education, not less. Yet the time was not ripe for action.

A few days later Theodore's father left town on business. Ann then
called the aspiring farmer into her presence and calmly announced that
he was being sent immediately to a classical school at Basking Ridge,
New Jersey, under the guidance of Rev. Robert Finley. Theodore was
"greatly vexed" by this revelation, but he had no recourse. She stood
her ground, and his father could not be reached. He packed up and departed for Basking Ridge. Later, of course, he came to see the wisdom of
his stepmother's decision.

1

Ann Frelinghuysen was a good Christian woman and, according to the expectations of the time, not inclined to challenge her husband's authority. What compelled her then to take such drastic action? Part of the answer lies, I believe, in her sensing of something special in Theodore. He was bright and articulate, despite his adolescent weariness with school. She sensed a potential in him that was not quite as evident in Frederick or in his older brother, John. Maybe, just maybe, Theodore would become a leader, one who could continue the Frelinghuysen tradition of Christian leadership in New Jersey and the Northeast.

Another key, then, was Ann's commitment to the Frelinghuysen family name and history. Young Theodore was already the fourth generation of New Jersey Frelinghuysens. The patriarch, Theodore Jacobus Frelinghuysen, emigrated to the colonies in 1720 from East Friesland and immediately took up his duties as an ordained minister in the Dutch Reformed Church. He was a powerful preacher whose reputation spread quickly among the Dutch of northern New Jersey. Theodore Jacobus believed in revival and preached accordingly. To say that he was "successful" as a revivalist would be an understatement. It would be closer to the truth to acclaim him as a key figure in the colonial phenomenon, the First Great Awakening. He was equal to other potent instruments of this spiritual quickening, such as Jonathan Edwards, Gilbert Tennent, and the English revivalist, George Whitefield. In fact, Theodore J. Frelinghuysen's preaching and pastoral work contributed significantly to making New Jersey a bastion of religious conservatism, the "garden" of the Dutch Reformed Church in the colonies in the eighteenth century.

Fittingly, the patriarch had a family of seven, five of whom were sons. All the sons chose to follow in their father's footsteps and were eventually ordained to the ministry. The second son, John, was a precocious youth, with a sincere religious faith. Upon reaching his maturity, he decided, together with many other Dutch Reformed young men, to travel to Holland for his theological training. Returning to New Jersey, he soon succeeded his father in the pastorate in 1750. Early signs indicated that John would be a popular and effective preacher; contemporaries praised him particularly for his facility with young people. He no doubt hoped to further the cause of the Great Awakening, just then beginning to lose its significance. This was not to be the case, however, because in 1754 at the age of twenty-five he died.

John left a young widow, Dinah, and two small children: a girl, Eva, and a boy, Frederick, who would later become Theodore's father. Dinah's desire was to see Frederick continue the Frelinghuysen tradition of pastoral leadership. She prayed and worked for this but to no avail. He was to make his name in the "secular" world. And what a name!

Here are a few of his accomplishments: He was a diligent student

2

- <u>True for</u>

(1) Tend to think
these Vey *different*
for *streets* spelly
<u>Chesun</u>

(Not)

at the College of New Jersey (now Princeton), mastering, among other things, the Hebrew language. (One of his classmates was James Madison.) Following college, he studied law and began a promising law practice. He quickly gained notoriety by supporting the cause of revolution against the British. As a reward for his spirit of rebellion, he was first chosen to join the Provincial Congress of New Jersey (1775), then three years later was made a member of the New Jersey delegation to the Continental Congress. Service in the Continental Congress was interrupted when he resigned to become a captain in the artillery. As a military officer he made valuable contributions to the crucial Revolutionary battles of Trenton and Monmouth. (According to rumor, he fired the shot that struck down the feared Hessian commander, Colonel Rahl.) Frederick eventually rose to the position of colonel in the militia and finally was commissioned major-general in the army by his friend, President Washington. A grateful New Jersey legislature appointed him United States senator in 1793, a position he held until 1796. At his death in 1804, he was lauded as one of New Jersey's greatest Revolutionary heroes and finest citizens.

Such an illustrious ancestral history was a source of great pride to Ann Frelinghuysen, and rightfully so. A sore spot remained, however, namely, the lack of sincere spirituality of the third generation hero, Frederick. His Christian commitment remained largely superficial; in fact, he was never received into full communicant membership in the church. Perhaps this was the final reason for Theodore's being whisked away during his father's absence.

Although no direct evidence exists, it is logical to assume that Ann's co-conspirator in this project was Dinah, Theodore's grandmother. If not, she certainly approved of Theodore's continuing education and had great hopes for his future as a Christian leader like his grandfather and great-grandfather before him.

After the death of her husband, John, Dinah had married Jacobus Hardenberg, a prominent cleric and educator. Dinah made him an excellent match, for her Christian life blossomed, and she came to be loved by all who knew her. Contemporaries praised here for her virtue, wisdom, and deep spirituality, affectionately calling her the "Jufvrouw Hardenberg," the loved and respected older woman.

Dinah, even more than Ann, molded the character of the young Theodore. She spent considerable time with her grandson, playing with him, teaching him, taking particular pains to point him in the direction of the Savior. Perhaps it was while sitting upon her knee that he also first heard of the Frelinghuysen heritage. Theodore never tired of speaking of his grandmother, who died when he was twenty, and how much he owed to her prayers and counsels.

The third potter who shaped the clay was Robert Finley of Basking Ridge. A more appropriate model could hardly have been found. Finley was Princeton-trained and chose teaching as his first vocation. His initial apprenticeship was in a grammar school supervised by the famous theologian-educator, John Witherspoon. After teaching for a time, he returned to Princeton to study theology under Witherspoon and to seek ordination in the Presbyterian Church. In 1795 he accepted a call to the Presbyterian Church at Basking Ridge, where he would serve for twenty-two years.

Burdened by the lack of good schools in the area, Finley soon opened his own classical academy for boys. His curriculum was a rigorous mixture of langauge study, history, moral philosophy, and theology. But pedagogy was only one side of Finley's ministry; he deeply loved each individual student. What a powerful witness in Theodore's life! Before long the resentment at not being allowed to be a farmer melted away, and he was thriving under Finley's tutelage. Later in life Theodore acknowledged a profound debt to his childhood teacher, giving him credit for much of his moral vision. In a subsequent chapter I will give one example of this indebtedness.

How did the young Theodore respond spiritually to the grace of God revealed to him directly and mediated through the three Christians just described? No doubt his stepmother and grandmother worried that he would follow his father's spiritual example rather than the model of John and Theodore Jacobus. But from Basking Ridge through college, Theodore gave outward signs of sincere Christian faith: familiarity with Scripture, attendance at church services, and personal holiness. Yet, something was missing; there seemed little spark to his faith, little excitement to his walk with God. Perhaps the women's worst fears were being realized. Friends noticed his reluctance to take a leadership role in appropriate church settings or to witness to others of his relationship to Christ. In his 1862 eulogy William Campbell recalled that the young scholar "did everything seemly and proper, except the one thing needful, he did not give his heart to Christ."

Despite lacking a spiritual heart, however, the outward signs continued to appear. In 1811 he helped establish the Second Presbyterian Church in Newark, serving on its first board of trustees and volunteering to work with the Sunday school. A few years later he made public profession of his faith and was received into full communicant membership. Thus, New Jersey's new attorney general in 1817 appeared to be not only a rising political star but also a man whose feet were firmly planted in the soil of evangelical conservative Christianity. But the core was still missing.

The turning point in Theodore's spiritual life occurred during November, 1820. On the twentieth of that month his younger brother, Frederick, died after a lingering illness. Frederick had been his childhood playmate, schoolmate, and closest friend. And their intimate relationship had continued into adolescence and early manhood. Naturally, the

4

death was traumatic to Theodore. But the events leading up to it and the manner of it had more impact that the death itself, for Frederick had recently accepted Christ into his life and renounced his own previous lukewarmness to the gospel. On his deathbed Frederick was telling everyone of the grace of the Savior whom he now served. When Theodore approached and asked what, exactly, Christ meant to him in his suffering, Frederick replied, ''Oh, Theodore, Theodore, I have not language to describe it. The enjoyment of this hour is greater than my whole life.'' When implored to refrain from speaking in order to conserve his strength, Frederick declared, ''Why? I am much happier than if I were asleep, and what I say may also do good hereafter.''

Theodore was transformed by his brother's death-bed testimony. According to his nephew, ''The impression it made upon Theodore was decided and indelible. It was so prevading as to render him, in the judgment of his friends, almost another man.'' A second contemporary noted that Theodore withdrew from public life for a week to meditate on his brother's death, discussing with friends its significance for his own future. The same friend, looking back from the perspective of many years, concluded, ''From that time down to his last moment on earth, the character of Theodore Frelinghuysen [had] a simplicity and singleness of goodness such as I have never seen in any other human being.'' A new man emerged in 1820, a new *Christian* man. ''Conversion'' had finally been the experience of New Jersey's attorney general. It is fair to say, in light of the labors of his stepmother and grandmother, that many prayers had been answered.

* * * * * * *

Discussion Questions

1. I suggested that Theodore's stepmother ''sensed'' certain leadership qualities in him. How can parents and adults accomplish this today? In other words, how do we recognize leadership potential in our children? Can this be done and still maintain family harmony? Isn't there a danger of playing favorites with our children?

2. If we fear that a child is only ''going through the motions'' with respect to his religious commitment, what kind of spiritual ''seeds'' can we plant which could sprout in the future? If the child also shows leadership potential, how would we change our planting strategy, i.e., would there be a different seeds to sow for such a child? Name them.

3. Theodore's stepmother was determined to continue his education. Today, we as a culture place even more emphasis on becoming educated. Yet, we still need to ask ourselves if education has been overrated. Just how crucial is formal education today for children? What level of education is important for a child with leadership potential? High school?

College? Graduate school? Would you be comfortable with a leader without a high school diploma? Without a college degree?

4. How important is spiritual maturity to effective leadership? In other words, do you feel it is important for leaders to have a fairly long period of spiritual growth before assuming leadership? Why or why not?

5. How important is it to to pray for the emergence of Christian leaders? Do you offer such prayers? How do we pray for leadership?

Chapter 2

New Jersey's Rising Star

> The insinuating eloquence by which the forensic efforts of
> Mr. Frelinghuysen were distinguished; his voice clear, mel-
> low, and full; his...brilliant imagination...fine flow of lan-
> guage, together with his acute knowledge of human nature,
> accurate legal acquirements, [and] strong reasoning pow-
> ers...rendered Mr. Frelinghuysen the most popular advocate
> at the Bar of Eastern New Jersey.
> —Cortlandt Parker, 1844

The year was 1812. Although a policy of "gradual" emancipation
had been adopted eight years previously in New Jersey, racism more
than lingered on. Blacks found few friends, apart from Quakers, in northern New Jersey. Most whites preferred simply to ignore them. What
would be the fate, then, of a black man who entered the public consciousness because he murdered a white man? Such was the situation
facing an unnamed black in that year, a penniless, friendless drifter.
Charged with murder, he pleaded self-defense, but being without financial
resources, he was unable to secure counsel. That the hangman's rope
awaited him aroused in the general public only "a morbid interest in
the [situation], but none for him."

Fortunately for the accused, the New Jersey court system provided
legal assistance for indigent cases. Even more fortunately, however,
the court appointed from a pool of already distinguished attorneys, Theodore Frelinghuysen.

The young lawyer did his homework. He appealed both to the act
of self-defense and to the sympathies of the court concerning his client's
condition. So expert was his presentation that the original racist bias
of the jury was undermined and the accused was promptly acquitted.
All who witnessed the trial were duly impressed by the young lawyer's
persuasiveness: "I never shall forget," recalled one typical observer,
"the impression made upon me by this address of Mr. Frelinghuysen....[Its impact] has never left me, and ever since I have regarded him with intense interest, from the feelings which his pathetic
eloquence then excited."

7

Actually, the court's choice of Theodore Frelinghuysen to defend a poor black man is not at all surprising. He was twenty-five years old in 1812 and already notable in the public arena. His reputation had spread throughout many Christian circles and within "polite" society in northern New Jersey. This was due in part, I believe, to the nature of his education and legal training.

Theodore finished his preparatory schooling at Basking Ridge in 1802. Since, by then, he had determined to continue his education, a proper college had to be chosen. Staying within the borders of New Jersey presented only two options for ambitious politicians: Queen's College (Rutgers) and the College of New Jersey (Princeton). He chose the latter and entered at the junior class level. Princeton turned out to be a propitious choice; it was not only an excellent college academically but also something of an elite training ground for New Jersey's aspiring leaders. For example, joining Frelinghuysen in the 1802 class were Philip Lindsley (future president of the University of Nashville), Samuel Southard (future judge and Theodore's colleague in the United States Senate), and Robert Ingersoll (future ambassador to England). It is important to note how Theodore functioned in his college years (1802-04) in such a highly charged environment.

All of Theodore's background pointed him toward a superb career as a Princeton undergraduate. Finley's rigorous curriculum and academic discipline had been what Theodore needed as preparation. As a result, he proved to be the ideal college student, diligent and always prepared in his studies. He simply didn't make "mistakes" in class because, as Ingersoll recalled, "With excellent abilities, great industry, suitable ambition, and never-failing attention, it could scarcely be otherwise. The studies were susceptible of being mastered, and he took care to conquer them." His was also a "liberal arts" triumph, for at Princeton he first developed a regimen of reading broadly. His favorites were Gibbon and Burke and the English classics, especially Milton and Shakespeare. It seemed altogether natural, then, for the college to select Frelinghuysen, the student leader, to deliver Princeton's valedictory address in 1804. No record of the address remains, but it was praised by teachers and students alike for its depth and for the oratorical style with which it was presented.

In 1804 Frelinghuysen's future was a promising one. Only the question of which profession to choose remained. After contemplating his prospects for a short time, he chose law. This choice is understandable for two reasons: the weakness of his religious commitment, which ruled out the ministry, and the example of his older brother, John, who had previously launched his own legal career. Besides, law was where service could be rendered and a reputation made, not insignificant items for a young man following his star.

During the early 1800's, "graduate training" in law came through an apprenticeship with a practicing attorney, first at the feet of his brother at the family home at Millstone (1804-08), then shortly later at the law office of Richard Stockton in Newark. Of the two, Stockton's influence was more substantial and long-lasting. A few observations, therefore, need to be made about this second phase.

A more distinguished master could hardly have been chosen. Richard (the "Duke") Stockton had practiced law successfully for more than twenty years and had even argued cases before the United States Supreme Court. He was a leading New Jersey politician who had been appointed to the United States Senate in 1796 to fill the remaining term of Theodore's father, Frederick, who had resigned for family and professional reasons. Richard served until 1799 but declined renomination in order to concentrate on his legal career and New Jersey politics. He soon launched a bid, ultimately unsuccessful, for New Jersey's governorship. Nonetheless, Stockton's formal and informal power in New Jersey was widely recognized. (From 1813 to 1815 he would serve a term in the United States House of Representatives.)

It appears that Stockton's greatest impact on his own trainee was in the area of politics and political philosophy. Stockton was New Jersey's premier Federalist, who adored the Constitution and the "federalism" it created. He clung tenaciously to this foundation, long after the Federalist party itself had collapsed as an ineffective alternative to the Democratic-Republican party of the Jeffersonians. The federalism of the Constitution always remained for him the "ark of safety" for individuals and the nation. "Religious" devotion to the Constitution and the federal system would be an accurate label to pin on Stockton's tenacity. Since Frelinghuysen's initial sympathies were also to the same federalism and to the Federalist party, it is fair to conclude that they came in part from his years spent under the supervision of Richard Stockton. This is an important point, for I hope to show in subsequent chapters the basic continuity of Frelinghuysen's political philosophy throughout his life.

Under the scrutiny of his brother and especially the "Duke," Frelinghuysen's legal training progressed smoothly until he was admitted to the bar in 1808, at age twenty-one. But legal preparation was only one aspect of his life during these years. He also found time, as would be his lifelong habit, to be involved in numerous other cultural pursuits, frequently as a leader. He organized, for example, a debate society for young men, encouraging them in their efforts at oratory, rhetoric, and the art of written communication. He may not have been talking to others about Christ during these years, but he was reaching out to people, making them a part of his life, which is indispensable as training for future leadership.

For the next two decades, Frelinghuysen immersed himself in his legal career and the cultural life of his home state. Such devotion paid rich dividends when the state legislature selected him for attorney general in 1817. His selection was not simply a political one—several Democratic-Republicans also voted for him—but because few other young attorneys had comparable records. He had not only won the sensational murder case involving the black man but had been involved in other precedent-setting trials as well, in Essex and several other New Jersey counties. Further, he had proven his dedication and patriotism in the War of 1812 by raising a volunteer company of riflemen and personally assuming command. Although it did not see active service, the people and the legislature did not forget the self-sacrificing action of its commander.

Frelinghuysen, as attorney general, served as the chief legal officer of the state. His responsibilities grew accordingly. In 1823 he lamented to a friend, "I am so constantly engaged in court, that I cannot keep up with my normal correspondence." Yet, like many leaders of any age, he seemed to flourish under the constraints of a busy schedule. Somehow his schedule neither kept him from increasingly active church work, which had been reinvigorated by his "conversion" in 1820, nor from initial involvement in the benevolent societies just beginning to take root in American soil. For example, colonization societies, Bible societies, and societies to aid the poor, all benefited from his energetic guidance during the decade of the 1820's. In fact, he made major addresses to all three types of societies (see bibliography).

What leadership qualities were exhibited by Frelinghuysen during these pre-senatorial years? A composite picture emerges when we examine the sketches of his contemporaries. In the first place, they all highlighted the power of his oratory. In an age when leaders depended almost entirely on vocalizing, Frelinghuysen was "Mr. Orator." Legal associates also pointed out his intuitive grasp of legal issues, the comprehensive nature of his knowledge, and his mastery of legal details and technicalities; as one friend noted, he mastered the details rather than vice versa. The rapid incisiveness of his legal judgment did not go unnoticed either. One colleague summarized his facility as follows:

> Whenever I had a case of difficulty or perplexity, I was in the habit of going to my friend A., my senior at the bar, for advice. He had a very fertile and ingenious mind, and would soon suggest half a dozen explanations or expedients to obviate the difficulty, but would not decide positively on any one of them. I would then go to Mr. Frelinghuysen. He at once would tell me which of them all was the true solution, and I never knew him to make a mistake.

Sociability was another of his commendable attributes. He loved people and enjoyed communicating with them in writing. This practice naturally affected his vocation; few lawyers, I believe, carried on the volume of professional correspondence attributed to Frelinghuysen.

Following the example of his mentor, Frelinghuysen also became a teacher during these years, a trainer of young lawyers. Apprentice students flocked to his office in anticipation of thorough professional preparation. Many called him "friend and father," according to his nephew, Talbot Chambers.

Finally, an acute sense of conscience and morality characterized his legal life. He yearned to see both a proper interaction between counselor and client and the truth emerge from the legal process. Laudable goals indeed. Perhaps, though, one reservation should be mentioned: At times, his morality verged on moral*ism*, an exaggerated expression of moral sensitivity. It was difficult for Frelinghuysen to separate his personal opinions about right and wrong from his conduct as an attorney. He would never accept, for example, a case involving a client whose action violated his own standard of ethics. "If I think him [a potential client] wrong," he asserted, "I send him to another lawyer." I would suggest that this was excessive on the part of Frelinghuysen. A strong moral consciousness did, nonetheless, combine with other factors to propel, inexorably, his ascending personal star in the 1820's.

And politics was never far from the mind of the attorney general, either. In fact, partly to keep his political options open, he declined the offer of the legislature in 1826 to a seat on the state Supreme Court. Legal and political service, he concluded, were more effectively rendered as attorney general than as a "disinterested" judge. During the 1820's, New Jersey politics was in flux. The Federalist party had virtually died out, but a viable two-party option had not yet emerged; it was an "era of good feelings," meaning that personalities rather than issues dominated political life (making it actually a time of "unremitting strife"). Frelinghuysen, the former Federalist, provided some leadership throughout this period of change, a time when everyone was called a Democratic-Republican. It primarily came in the support of the personal fortunes of John Quincy Adams, whom he believed held principles closer to his own than Adams' chief rival, Andrew Jackson. He thus became a strong Adams man in 1824—happy in the presidential victory—and continued his support through 1828 when he was disappointed in the loss of the presidency to Jackson.

The year 1826 is an important date because it marked the first entry of Frelinghuysen into the political arena. He sought to capitalize upon his loyalty to Adams by gaining the senatorial nod from the Adams-dominated state legislature. In that year Senator Joseph McIlvaine died, necessitating a replacement. Frelinghuysen vied for the appointment with Ephraim Bateman, a state legislator. It was a very close election, a cliffhanger. Bateman won, but only because he cast the deciding ballot for himself! No record exists of Frelinghuysen's response to Bateman's action, though many others expressed dismay at such questionable conduct. Today's scholars have concluded that Frelinghuysen was "clearly the more able of the two."

The attorney general returned to his duties and kept a low profile for the next two years. He surfaced again politically in 1828 when he became actively involved in the reelection bid of President Adams. He worked diligently for the Adams cause, being chosen, for example, as an Adams elector from Essex county in the February convention in Trenton. Adams lost his bid, but, happily for Frelinghuysen, he carried New Jersey. This time his dedication paid off: following the election, he was appointed by the legislature as United States senator.

Now he could bring his developing Christian vision to Washington.

* * * * * * *

Discussion Questions

1. Frelinghuysen risked his reputation and career by giving legal assistance to the black man in 1812. How much does leadership require in terms of similar courageous stands? Or is it more a matter of a quiet resolve, working behind the scenes? Or a mixture of both? Describe an act of courageous leadership which you have noticed lately.

2. Frelinghuysen became immersed in his work as an attorney and as the state's attorney general. Does leadership by definition require such commitment of time and energy? What dangers exist when extraordinary devotion is given to a career, especially an important public one? How can we, as evangelicals, help relieve the "burden of office" from our leaders? Name a few specific ways we can help.

3. We want our leaders to be men and women of conscience, of moral sensitivity. Yet, I've suggested that morality can become moral*ism*. What is the danger of moralism in leadership? Can you give examples from present leaders of moral concern becoming moralism? What about the subject of "single issue" politics; to what extent is it moralism?

4. In understanding Frelinghuysen it is necessary to place him in his historical and political context. This is also true of us as evangelicals as we assess true leadership today. What are the political contours of your immediate surroundings? Is it a healthy two-party context or a one-party rule? Is it liberal or conservative or moderate? Would you support a third party, beyond Republicans or Democrats? Do evangelicals in your area become active politically? If not, what do you think is the reason? What could be done to change that politically apathetic attitude?

5. Frelinghuysen lost his bid for the Senate but apparently did not let this defeat make him bitter. There is a lesson in his response worth remembering. How do we evangelicals handle repeated defeats in politics or in other battles where leadership is crucial? What attitudes are necessary for us evangelicals to keep ourselves from despondency when confronted by repeated defeats and "hopeless causes"?

6. Name a young political leader today whose career has impressed you. What qualities does he or she have which attract you?

Chapter 3

Here I Stand

He was a statesman. He took large views of things. He looked
beyond present emergencies and acted for the future.
                    —Talbot Chambers on Frelinghuysen, 1863

Defeat in such a cause [defense of Indian rights] is far above
the triumphs of unrighteous power—and in the language of
an eloquent writer—"I had rather receive the blessing of one
poor Cherokee, as he casts his last look back upon his country, for having, though in vain, attempted to prevent his
banishment, than to sleep beneath the marble of all the
Caesars."
                    —Theodore Frelinghuysen in the Senate, 1830

The year was 1834 and the political stakes were high. President Jackson
had decided to destroy the "evil monster," the Second Bank of the United
States (BUS), whose charter was due to expire in 1836. He had announced his intentions in the presidential campaign of 1832, and after
his victory he proceeded to carry out his threat by removing government deposits and placing them in "pet banks" in various states. By
1834 it had become a bloody battle as the "giants" of the Senate—
including Henry Clay and Daniel Webster—marshalled their forces in
support of the BUS against a stubborn, popular, and politically powerful president.

It was also a crucial personal test for Senator Theodore Frelinghuysen
of New Jersey. He had clearly cast his lot with the "loyal opposition"
to Jackson, the emerging National-Republican party of Clay and Webster (soon to be renamed the Whig party). In fact, he was a leading congressional opponent of Jackson on the bank issue, in many ways the
spokesman of the allied opposition forces. It was exhilarating to be in
such company, but a dark cloud had recently appeared on the horizon,
causing him to pause and ponder his future.

That cloud was the political reality of his home state. The Jacksonians, or Democrats as they were now called, had gained control of the
New Jersey legislature. Under Jackson's spell, the state party came out
in strong support of the crusade to crush the BUS. The legislature quickly

15

informed both senators that they were to suppress any vocal opposition to the president; in fact, they were ordered to affirm him with their votes!

Senator Frelinghuysen deliberated only a short time. In January, 1834, he arose in a hushed Senate to deliver his response to his state legislature's mandate:

> Sir, my instructions require me to sustain by my vote and influence "the course of the Secretary [of the Treasury]." The conclusions [however] are erroneously drawn from mistaken premises. I dissent from the whole plea, the beginning, middle and end of the matter.

He had defied the state legislature, choosing conscience over expediency! In a few months he would discover what it meant for his political future.

But what did Frelinghuysen's immediate past look like in 1834? His was an impressive record. He had arrived on the scene in 1829 determined to be a force for morality and righteousness and immediately sought to transform his dream into reality. He thus became involved in most of the important issues of his day, frequently, I will show, as a leader.

And his leadership was not, contrary to Arthur Schlesinger, Jr., and others, negative or reactionary in nature. His opposition to Jackson, for example, should not be regarded merely as a "foolish" denial of a strong executive. He could, and did, support the executive when the situation demanded it. The "Nullification Crisis" of 1832 is a case in point. During this crisis, involving a Southern threat of secession if tariff rates were not lowered, the senator sided with the president's adamant opposition to secession. Jackson's "Force Bill"—whereby he threatened military intervention against a rebellious South—was also supported by Frelinghuysen. The use of executive power to confront sovereign states was seen by him as the only recourse in light of "the absurd doctrine of Nullification." In short, "reactionary" would be an unfair label to pin on the New Jersey senator. Far more than reacting against, he was *standing for* something, *for* a government and a program with definite features; and he must be judged accordingly.

I find it helpful to summarize Frelinghuysen's political philosophy as one which stressed four interrelated themes: 1) compassionate statism, 2) Christian confessionalism, 3) justice, and 4) federalism. What follows is an examination of some of the issues related to these themes as they surfaced during his years in Washington.

Compassionate Statism

I don't mean to suggest by "compassionate statism" that Frelinghuysen was a socialist; no one would make such a claim, then or now. He did, however, transcend the narrow framework of a "laissez-faire" approach

16

to the role of government in the life of the nation, the typical approach of the Jacksonian Democrats. A "limited" government in the laissez-faire sense was simply not adequate in his mind. The great truth of our political experiment, he declared in 1831, lay in the undeniable fact "that government was only so far rightful, as it sought the welfare of the whole: that it was to be maintained not for the advancement of the few, over the neglected rights of the many, but to secure and to reserve to all the people, the sacred rights of life, liberty and property." In order for the welfare of the whole to be realized, the state had to act as a positive force in national life. The Democratic program of individualism and unguided market forces, he believed, would cause much social and economic misery.

A good example of Frelinghuysen's political compassion can be seen in his approach to pension relief. Pension bills creating certain kinds of relief for veterans of the American Revolution had been hotly debated in Congress in 1818 and again in 1826. In the early 1830's, Senator Frelinghuysen became a leader in renewed efforts to revise and expand national pension coverage for veterans. He was particularly disturbed by two features of previous laws: 1) the requirement that to receive aid veterans had to confess publicly their "absolute poverty," and 2) the invidious distinction made between the regular army and the militia. He challenged both humiliating features and supported efforts for their eradication via new legislation. To do otherwise was to ignore, shamefully, the inestimable contributions of those brave men who had "staked all" for the glorious cause of independence.

The need for a compassionately active national government most clearly appeared in the senator's support of the "American System" of Henry Clay. Throughout his years in Washington, Frelinghuysen worked in concert with Clay and other National-Republicans to develop and implement a program of federally sponsored subsidies of "home industries" and "internal improvements"—roads, canals, harbors, etc. These efforts were to be financed through tariffs and the sale of public lands. This "activist" view of the role of the state was vigorously opposed by the Democrats. They regarded the American System as a serious departure from the revealed truths of laissez-faire and as a threat to the sacred freedom of the individual. Frelinghuysen, on the other hand, believed that

> to foster the mechanical skill, genius and industry of our own people, with the cotton and iron and timber at our very door, was among the clearest dictates of political wisdom. That honest labor here might always find employment, and never want bread, nor the means to earn it, was the plainest duty, as well as the purest patriotism.

In short, government encouragement of home industry and internal improvements, in the context of stiff competition from England and elsewhere, was necessitated by both logic and compassion.

In retrospect, Frelinghuysen's support of an active, positively involved government put him on the vanguard of political reform in his age. It took courage to champion an activist state in face of the laissez-faire convictions so prevalent in antebellum America. Today, almost all of us believe in the "American System." Who would seriously propose, for example, either the withdrawal of federal support for the national highway system, the railroad system, and other "internal improvements," or the abrogation of the moral duty of the government to uplift those individuals who are truly in need? We now recognize, thanks in part to men like Clay and Frelinghuysen, that the state can and must work, positively, for the general welfare.

Christian Confessionalism

I have in mind by the term "Christian confessionalism" the efforts of Senator Frelinghuysen to have the government acknowledge publicly the sovereignty of God over America and her dependence on divine providence. This did not imply theocracy, as some have charged, but something quite different. At a later point I will examine in depth his particular belief that America was a Christian nation; here, I only wish to deal with the expression of a broader, less arguable issue.

Frelinghuysen's assertion that America needed to confess the "obvious" is apparent when looking first at his approach to natural disasters. In 1832, for example, he strongly concurred with a resolution initiated by Henry Clay to call upon God's mercy in the wake of the scourge of cholera which was then sweeping across America. The resolution asked for a day of humiliation, fasting, and prayer in which supplications could be humbly offered for divine relief from the terrible epidemic.

In his Senate testimony, Frelinghuysen referred to a similar joint resolution proposed and passed in 1812, at the outset of the war with England. He felt the need to call upon precedent, because the idea of a resolution concerning the epidemic was experiencing stiff opposition, especially in the House. Several congressmen had gone on record as opposing the "Christian resolution," since America was a secular state. Religion, they agreed, should be separate from secular politics. (How modern the sound!) The senator's response to such a dichotomy is worth quoting at length:

> I hope, sir, that the resolution may meet with no serious
> opposition [in the Senate]. It surely becomes us to ac-
> knowledge our dependence, and to implore the interposition
> of God's mercy in this season of alarm. The Constitution
> can present no obstacle, for it is not an exercise of political
> power. It is far beyond the range of politics. It is an act of

18

> piety to God, becoming a whole nation; in which rulers and
> people are invited...to bow together before the throne of
> grace...[and] unite in one common supplication to Him...that
> He would spare us in this day of his righteous judgment.

The resolution carried in the Senate thirty to thirteen, but, regrettably, failed in the House.

The Clay-Frelinghuysen "confession" was, I believe, an appropriate stand for at least two reasons: 1) it was Biblical, stating the simple truth that America depends on God's grace, and 2) it required a governmental response to a crisis, not a binding one, but a public, moral confession nonetheless. It is comforting to note that many similar resolutions have been offered since the days of Frelinghuysen, and some have passed.

The senator's paramount stand for a national confession, however, involved the even more controversial issue of Sunday mail. In 1810 Congress had passed a bill requiring the transportation and delivery of mail seven days a week. The Christians' response was swift, as subsequent repeal petitions swamped Congress. But the early petitions arrived haphazardly, without intelligent planning; consequently, little action occurred. In 1828 and 1829 a more concerted effort unfolded, with Theodore Frelinghuysen as moral leader. In May, 1830 Frelinghuysen introduced his resolution to repeal the 1810 law. He did so because, as he declared in the preamble, "The Sabbath is justly regarded as a divine institution...[and] no legislature can rightfully reject its claims...[nor] should not, by positive legislation, encroach upon the sacredness of this day, or weaken its authority in the estimate of the people."

A furious battle followed, with Congressman Richard Johnson of Kentucky leading the assault against the repeal effort. Johnson's argument centered on two points: 1) that repealing the existing law would create economic hardship among businessmen, and 2) that the crucial doctrine of the separation of church and state was threatened by Frelinghuysen's bill. Sabbatarians sought a "religious despotism," he concluded abusively. The senator from New Jersey responded at length but not in kind.

The Christian senator quickly rejected both of Johnson's contentions. Some "profits" might be diminished, he acknowledged, but our true worth as a people came from a peaceful conscience and moral excellence. No monetary valuation could be placed on such virtues.

The allegation of religious despotism was dismissed as a perversion of the real meaning of the separation doctrine. Theocracy did not enter into the picture. In fact, Frelinghuysen turned the tables completely, arguing that the petitioners against the existing law were the true defenders of religious liberty! Only they understood the foundational principles at work in a constitutional republic.

Frelinghuysen could make such a case only on the basis of a broader view of religion than the popular one which had emerged in post-

Enlightenment America. According to the Enlightenment view, religion was largely a personal matter, a private concern between a man and his god. Among institutions, only the church could be regarded as a proper arena of religious activity. Frelinghuysen rejected this completely. "It is a most dangerous and destructive delusion," he argued, "to suppose that although as individuals and families, we are bound to respect the principles of religion, yet when we assume the character of States and Nations they cease to exert any legitimate influence." Both individuals and states owed God religious allegiance, each in its own way, yet complementarily.

What did governmental allegiance to the sovereignty of God imply for Frelinghuysen? Simply a recognition of the Sabbath as a divine institution, created by God for man's enjoyment, for rest, worship, and acts of goodness. "Ordinary" business should be discouraged, as well as mass public entertainment. And when government made such a "confession," great rewards followed closely, not just moral rewards, but material ones as well. We had, thus, everything to gain and nothing to lose, he felt, by overturning the Sunday mail law.

The senator strengthened his argument in 1830 by numerous citations of English law, American state laws, and congressional and judicial precedents. He also invoked the rights of the "majority" to determine public policy in a democracy. It was a comprehensive response to the charges of sensationalism made by his opponents.

In the final analysis, the majority proved elusive; the Frelinghuysen bill lost in Congress. Perhaps the public was not as aroused as he believed; perhaps the forces of secularism were too strong in his day. Repeal of Sunday mail delivery would have to wait for another day. I believe, nonetheless, that his efforts were progressive and insightful. His confessional stance recognized the duty of government to be sensitive to the broader meaning of the Moral Law and opened new vistas for exploring the definitions of religion, church, and state. Frelinghuysen was, in my experience, one of the first evangelicals to understand the difference between separation of church and state and separation of religion *from* the state. Few other distinctions are as important as this one.

Justice

Defense of Indian rights [i.e., the Cherokees] earned Senator Frelinghuysen more notoriety than any other issue in the 1830's. According to Chambers, his stance made his name a "household word" among evangelical Christians. Abolitionist William Lloyd Garrison even wrote a poem in honor of the freshman senator upon hearing of Frelinghuysen's activity. Garrison pictured Frelinghuysen as a "meek soldier of the Cross," a "Patriot and Christian" whose presence in the Senate was politically indispensable.

Familiarity, however, did not create unanimity. A substantial amount of hostility existed within Christian circles to the New Jersey senator's position. Many Christians, for racial, economic, and theological reasons, defended removal of the Indians to lands west of the Mississippi. Importantly, the Dutch Reformed leadership—Frelinghuysen's ancestral church—generally supported Jackson's policy on the Cherokees. Naturally, many national political figures agreed: Senator Thomas Hart Benton, for example, condemned the efforts of Frelinghuysen and other reformers as "political and pseudo-philanthropic intermeddling" with something that was none of their business.

In light of its controversial nature and the degree of overall opposition, why did Frelinghuysen single out this issue only months after arriving in Washington? I believe the answer is obvious: it was his uncompromising concern for justice. First and foremost, Indian rights was a matter of simple justice, a matter of political morality. Politics must conform to a higher standard than expediency; it must even be color blind, he intimated. "Do the obligations of justice change with the color of the skin?" he asked his fellow senators. No! was his resounding answer.

The new senator used several tactics in his crusade. One strategy involved assuming the role of gadfly to the administration. Thus, he frequently asked for information from the White House on Indian policy in an effort to catch them in an embarrassing contradiction or outright error. If nothing else, his bites kept the administration from taking the Senate for granted on this issue. In addition, Frelinghuysen had learned another tactic by observing the English evangelicals in their battles to end the slave trade and for emancipation, namely, the use of petitions. Following their example, he initiated a campaign to flood the Senate Indian Affairs committee with petitions calling for the transformation of administration policy. That they had less effect in the United States than the evangelicals had in England does not detract from the efforts of the man who regarded himself as an American Wilberforce.

Frelinghuysen's most effective tactic was public pronouncement, the capstone of which came in his Senate speech of April 6, 1830. In 1829 the state of Georgia had passed a bill which, for all practical purposes, forced the Cherokee tribe to abandon its homeland and begin the long trek west. Congress, with Jackson's blessing, followed suit in 1830. When Frelinghuysen rose to speak on April 6, he was actually offering an amendment to the bill under discussion, hoping to modify it in favor of the legal and moral rights of the Cherokees. His amendment had three central provisions: 1) that any relocation must be truly voluntary; 2) that until they moved or if they stayed, all their legal rights must be honored; and 3) that if they moved, new treaties must be established fully guaranteeing their rights in their new lands west of the Mississippi. Needless to say, this was not what Georgia or Jackson had in mind.

The 1830 speech deserves examination. What follows are some of the themes worth noting.

Frelinghuysen proclaimed that the only purpose of the Georgia bill was the outright removal of the Cherokees. No pretense of evenhandedness in the legislation could be assumed. It left the Cherokees with few or no options. In fact, many of its provisions were "wicked." Three were especially obnoxious to the senator. The first made it illegal to establish any barriers to Cherokee emigration. In practice this would mean, he predicted, that people could be prosecuted for encouraging them to stay. The second evil provision forbade Indians from testifying against whites in state court (unless the whites lived in Indian territory). Frelinghuysen, the Christian lawyer, could not hide his contempt for this feature, calling it a "wretched" provision that would encourage roving bands of whites to violate Indian territory with impunity. Finally, the Georgia bill in effect annulled laws and ordinances passed by the Cherokees in previous decades. They became null and void, as if they had never existed. Human history, he lamented, had never witnessed such "high-handed usurpation."

Georgia's immorality, Frelinghuysen declared, was obvious to anyone who understood history and law. He summarized the injustice as follows: 1) The Cherokees had original title to the land, for they were a free, independent, and sovereign tribe. As individuals, they possessed "kindred faculties and powers with ourselves," which entitled them to share in God's bounty. 2) Cherokee tribal government had always been an effective political force, a fairly sophisticated instrument of public policy. They were not barbarians. 3) The Cherokees had long maintained a policy of open-handed friendship with whites, especially with Georgia's authorities. 4) They had always met their legal obligations to Georgia, rarely faltering from faithful observance of past formalities. In short, the land belonged to them, and they could not be removed without their permission. The greed of the white man should not prevail!

Frelinghuysen then pointed out that the Indian dilemma was not essentially a state issue anyway, since the Constitution gave original jurisdiction to the federal government. According to the Constitution, Indian tribes were sovereign powers requiring formal treaties as the basis of legal intercourse. And only the federal government had treaty power, a power which they had historically applied in good faith in their past dealings with the Cherokees.

Frelinghuysen then sketched the history of treaty relations with the Cherokees—a very satisfying one, in his opinion. He noted with pride the 1791 Treaty of Holston wherein perpetual friendship with the Indians was affirmed and definite boundaries were cited. He cited the treaties of 1809 and 1817 where Georgia's Indians, as Frelinghuysen worded it, would continue to be treated as "a distinct and separate community, governed by their own peculiar laws and customs." Further, he pointed out that these treaties were built upon the solid foundation of legal documents created during the period of the Articles of Confederation and augmented throughout our history by special commercial legislation. In light of this history, he concluded, it was a "subject of wonder" that anyone still believed the Cherokees to be a part of Georgia, subject to her laws.

President Jackson did, prompting another Frelinghuysen volley. Jackson, he regretted, was not Washington. In fact, Old Hickory had abandoned not only Washington's honorable policy toward the Indians but the precedents established by all our previous presidents. Since in the American system ultimate enforcement of treaties rested with the executive, the discontinuity spelled disaster for the Cherokees. The president's "executive disposition" also signaled a grave crisis for America: "No one branch of the Government can rescind, modify, or explain away our public treaties. They are the supreme law of the land, so declared to be by the Constitution. They bind the President and all other departments, rulers, and people." By implication, Jackson and Georgia were conspiring to undermine the Constitution itself.

The final irony involved the lifestyle of the Cherokee nation. Of all the Indian tribes, he reminded his listeners, they had become the most assimilated into the American way of life. They possessed not only a civil government and wise laws but also a printing press, a weekly newspaper, schools, and Christian churches. The Cherokees had made remarkable progress in cultural and moral cultivation, to the point where they could live as productive neighbors with the white man. How ironic, he noted, that we would now refuse to acknowledge them by honoring our treaties with them.

The Christian senator concluded his argument with the bold assertion that both the "unchangeable principles of justice" and the dictates of our good name required rejection of the Jackson-Georgia innovations. The situation was really quite simple: the Cherokees had always met their treaty obligations; "they now expect from a great People, the like fidelity to plighted covenants." "Sir," he warned, "if this law be enforced, I do religiously believe that it will awaken tones of feeling that will go up to God and call down the thunder of His wrath."

The final vote was a disappointment to Frelinghuysen; it passed by narrow margins in both houses. In subsequent years he continued the battle, but the tide was against him. America soon grew weary of talk about "Indian rights." The country had a continent to conquer and didn't look kindly on obstacles in its path. God's wrath seemed a distant thunder.

I judge the Indian rights issue as the moral high point of Frelinghuysen's years in Washington. His stance for justice rightly earned for him the title of America's Christian statesman. Critics would do well to heed the poetic tribute of William Lloyd Garrison:

Yet, Frelinghuysen! gratitude is due thee,
    And loftier praise than language can supply:
Guilt may denounce, and Calumny pursue thee,
    And pensioned Impudence they worth decry;
Brilliant and pure, Posterity shall view thee
    As a fair planet in a troublous sky.

Federalism

The most controversial issue in New Jersey politics from 1832 to 1834 was the fate of the Second Bank of the United States, the BUS. The Democrats carried statewide elections in 1833 and 1834 by making opposition to the "monster" a central plank of their platform. In 1834 the situation and controversy heightened as New Jersey suffered a severe economic recession. Democrats blamed the recession on the BUS; the National-Republicans blamed the decline on Jackson's hostility to the BUS.

Frelinghuysen, as I have noted, risked his political future by supporting the BUS. He did so because of a firm—perhaps "religious"—commitment to the principles of federalism. His January 1834 Senate speech is a good place to see his commitment at work.

By 1834 Jackson had already begun the process of removing deposits from the BUS and placing them in state banks. The process, however, had not been smooth. He had ordered his treasury secretary to remove the funds; the secretary had refused and was fired. A second secretary had been given the same order and suffered the same fate. Neither had agreed with the president's assessment of the monster. A third secretary, Roger B. Taney (of Dred Scot infamy), acquiesced and began removing the funds. When Frelinghuysen rose to speak, he was responding to a statement from Taney which defended the removal.

Frelinghuysen's argument had two dimensions, the popular-existential and the philosophical. On the existential side, he offered three reasons for supporting the BUS. First, the bank should be continued because it was created by our founding fathers in 1791 (The First Bank of the United States). They obviously didn't believe it was a monster; neither should Americans in the 1830's. In this context Frelinghuysen was particularly appreciative of the work of Alexander Hamilton, whom he called "a mind without superior in the political history of our country." Second, the people generally approved of the BUS, despite what the Democrats claimed. He was confirmed in this belief by numerous letters of encouragement, like the one he received in March, 1834, from James Davison:

> I am highly pleased with the manly and independent course
> you have taken. Many of the people...speak in high terms
> of approbation of [you]. I am told they say you...are an or-

> nament to the state and to the United States. Let me say to
> you, go on firmly. Your cause is good...May divine good-
> ness in much mercy deliver us from such an administration.

Third, the bank was successful, creating a sound currency at a crucial time of national expansion. In contrast, state banks were unable to do a good job, being inherently speculative and shaky, as history was proving. They were a recipe for economic disaster.

On the philosophical side, the Constitution was the fundamental law of the land and federalism its finest principle. This contention is nowhere more apparent than in the following portion of his 1834 speech:

> It is the federalism of the Constitution that I honor—the sys-
> tem of fundamental law, as expounded by Hamilton, Madi-
> son, and Jay, and administered by Washington, and most
> of his successors. I never drank at any other fountain, and
> wish to follow no other guide....It is, indeed, sir, a copious
> and perennial fountain, copious to supply all the social and
> political wants of this great confederacy, and of vital ener-
> gy fully adequate to impart its rich benefits still wider, as
> the lines of our Union shall expand and encompass many
> more noble States.

He further elaborated on federalism using the key doctrine of the separation of powers into legislative, executive, and judicial branches. "The great principles of our Government refer to its three Departments," he said, "and many blessings have come our way because of faithful adherence to this tripartite arrangement." According to Frelinghuysen, this separation doctrine applied to the controversy raging around the BUS in four ways: 1) It stimulated discussion on all issues of a nonfundamental nature. In other words, differences of opinion on a topic like the BUS should be expected in a tripartite government that has its power spread equally among three branches. In fact, such a difference of opinion among the branches should be encouraged for the health of the democracy. 2) It created a moral and legal obligation on the part of the Senate to investigate the president and cabinet officials. In so arguing, Frelinghuysen drew upon the "checks and balances" element of the doctrine. 3) It implied that the Senate must concur before a cabinet official is removed; the Senate voted to confirm, it must also vote to replace. 4) It implied that all three departments of government were equally responsible to obey not only the Constitution but the positive law of the land, i.e., statutes. Thus, all the details of the law establishing the charter for the BUS must be honored by each branch of government. Failure to do so would be a breach of positive law and a denial of the separation doctrine, consequently a threat to the Constitution itself.

Jackson was such a threat in Frelinghuysen's mind. The president's conduct horrified him; it was purely arbitrary, "executive encroachment" at its worst, the act of a Caesar or a Napoleon. Why? Because he violated all four meanings of the separation doctrine as just described. According to the senator, the president sought to squash discussion on the BUS, deny the right of investigation to the Senate, dismiss cabinet officials at will without Senate concurrence, and thumb his nose at the law, thus imperiling our fundamental law. On the fourth point, Frelinghuysen was quite adamant. The law establishing the charter gave the treasury secretary power over the BUS "provided that Congress should become the ultimate tribunal to review his conduct"—the Congress, he reiterated, not the president. Further, the law allowed the secretary to remove funds only when there was a violation of the charter. No violation had occurred. Even the third secretary, he claimed, could find no wrongdoing on the part of director Nicholas Biddle or the bank itself. Yet, the funds were being removed, and it was a "blow to the majesty of the law, aimed by the hand appointed to maintain and defend it." He could only conclude, "Men see that laws are become dead letters, and that *discretion* rules the country."

What evaluations can be made concerning his commitment to the BUS and federalism? I have little problem with the former. The country needed central banking to provide financial stability, whatever the particular structure. Frelinghuysen was therefore a visionary in sensing the need for a specific structural solution. However, his application of federalism as one dimension of his overall political philosophy is another matter. It was the weak link in the political chain. His notion of federalism, correctly, did acknowledge the three functions of government, but it tended to separate them too radically, making one department—the legislature—almost an antagonist of the other two. From Frelinghuysen's point of view, the executive naturally became the enemy, the branch to be opposed, the person (Jackson) to battle. Little harmony could therefore exist, especially when this structural tension combined with the natural hostilities which existed in the emerging two-party framework. Of course, federalism could be defended constitutionally; Frelinghuysen certainly did. But maybe that made it even more difficult for him to think critically about the antagonism implicit in his own perspective.

Frelinghuysen's commitment to federalism was not a problem in 1834: everyone defended the system then. His "mistake" was choosing to make his stance on the BUS. The choice was courageous because he knew the perspective of the New Jersey legislature. But it was politically unwise, for the legislature read his action as outright insubordination and immediately set course to unseat him in the fall. All the Democrats had to do was to retain control of the legislature (New Jersey had annual elections at the time), then choose a different senator to represent their wishes. Unfortunately, the legislature won the battle and replaced Frelinghuysen with a more malleable senator in 1835. But the conflict involving the BUS is only half of the story of Frelinghuysen's term as senator. The other half remains to be told.

26

* * * * * * *

Discussion Questions

1. Frelinghuysen wanted the state to be compassionately active, providing some direct services (pensions, for example) and many indirect business subsidies. Do you think this is wise? Would it lead inevitably to socialism? Where would you draw the line?

2. Frelinghuysen supported the idea of congressional resolutions whereby the government would confess publicly that America owed obedience to God and depended on His providence. Should this be done today in light of our more pluralistic and secular society? Name a situation in which such a confession would be appropriate today or in recent history.

3. What about "blue laws" like the Sunday mail restrictions sought by the senator? Should evangelicals fight to preserve them, at least at the local level? Name a specific situation where such a law exists or should be enacted and defend your reasons for saying so. Is the church-state separation doctrine threatened by these kinds of laws?

4. If "religion," as Frelinghuysen argued, cannot be separated from the state, how do we protect the rights of religious minorities? In other words, how much "religion" should we expect from the state?

5. Frelinghuysen defended the rights of Indians on the basis of justice for minorities. How can this principle be expanded today? Should minorities even have "special" protections? If so, name some and defend your choice.

6. Was Frelinghuysen a progressive on the need for central banking, a man far ahead of his time? Do you feel that the government should function as the primary central bank? Again, is political control of money dangerous, a move toward socialism?

7. What do you think of federalism as a political principle? Name some positive features and some negative ones. What other political options exist to federalism? Are any of these options more normative or practical?

Chapter 4

Statesmanship and "Friendly Persuasion"

[In the Senate] he always seemed self-poised, and bore himself uniformly with great ability and dignity. There was a vein of benignity and piety running through all his conduct and speeches which was refreshing and delightful to contemplate.

—Henry Clay on Frelinghuysen

He was captivated with the pride of originating a new system and with being the founder of a new sect....He would strike out a new path—he would raise a structure by which he might get himself a name....

—Frelinghuysen on Elias Hicks, 1833

As we have been implying, New Jersey was convulsed by politics in 1834. Any remnants of "good feelings" evaporated as partisanship erupted over the BUS and the recession, state sponsorship of river canals and the role of corporations in American life, and other issues. A new two-party framework was emerging, with the National-Republicans becoming the Whigs and the Jacksonians firmly attaching the Democratic label to themselves. The battle lines were drawn, and the Senate seat—Frelinghuysen's seat—was the focal point of the irrepressible conflict.

It was in this context that Frelinghuysen took the bold step of announcing his candidacy early in 1834. Normally, candidates waited longer; a two-month duration for the entire campaign was not unusual for this time in history. But the political turmoil, he believed, required swift action. In April he appeared before the National-Republican/Whig convention in Trenton to state his intentions. The convention greeted him warmly, confirmed his candidacy, and defended his duty to defy a legislature which did not, in its opinion, truly represent the wishes of the people of New Jersey. The Democrats, on the other hand, met to condemn Frelinghuysen (and Senator Samuel Southard, who had also defied the legislature on the bank issue).

During the next few months, the pace and rhetoric of the campaign grew geometrically, as both sides endeavored to win support of the electorate. Democrats held numerous meetings around the state attacking Frelinghuysen's stand on the bank, claiming it proved his elitism and lack of concern for representative government. Frelinghuysen also took to the streets, campaigning vigorously for reelection (reappointment). His message was the opposite one, i.e., he knew better than the legislature the will of the people—a risky but necessary ploy in light of the Democrats' campaign. In short, emotions ran high as both sides donned a democratic mantle.

Frelinghuysen's early announcement and hard campaigning were signs, I believe, of substantial uneasiness on his part about the upcoming campaign. But why did he have so much apprehension? Was it because of the people's response to the style and quality of his senatorial leadership?

The answer to this latter question can only be a negative one. All evidence points to a continuing popularity among the general citizenry, especially evangelicals. Although Frelinghuysen's name was probably not a "household word" among evangelicals, many loved him and the leadership he was providing in the Senate. Contemporary politicians also respected his leadership. Henry Clay's praise of his "great ability" in the Senate received seconds from Daniel Webster and John Randolph of Virginia, among others. Edward Everett of Massachusetts, for example, stated that Frelinghuysen was always listened to with "deference" in the Senate. According to Talbot Chambers, even President Jackson admired his principled opposition.

So what then of his practical effectiveness as a senator? One modern scholar, Joseph Folsom, says that Frelinghuysen's obvious leadership qualities led his contemporaries to conclude "that there was no man in Washington...who more potently affected the progress of events." In terms of concrete legislation, this was, no doubt, an exaggeration. He had lost the battles for Indian rights, Sunday mail restrictions, and the recharter of the BUS, for example. But he achieved success, nonetheless, in a variety of other legislative endeavors, including pension reform, the Nullification Crisis of 1832, and Clay's famous Compromise Tariff of 1833. On this basis, we would have to conclude that as a practical legislator Frelinghuysen was moderately successful.

Admiration for Frelinghuysen was appropriate because he did blossom as a leader during his years in the senate; he did become a "Christian statesman." Four characteristics of this statesmanship are worth noting. First, he proved to be a politically independent thinker and actor in the Senate. As Chambers stated, "[Although] habitually acting with the opponents of the administration, he never hesitated to differ from them rather than violate his own sense of right." Examples would include the Indian rights and Sunday mail controversies where his position received less than enthusiastic political support. Second, socia-

30

bility and cordiality continued to characterize his style of leadership. His sharp words against Jackson were an exception to his otherwise gracious and dignified demeanor in the Senate. *Ad hominem* arguments were not a part of his repertoire. Third, he emerged as the Senate's principal moral leader. One recent American history text claims that he was the only serious evangelical in the Senate during these years. I am not sure about such a claim, but Frelinghuysen was certainly *the* moral leader among Christians. No one equaled him as a champion for the moral and religious issues which we highlighted in the previous chapter. Fourth, his communicative skills continued to shine brightly. I have in mind, initially, his oratorical power. Having developed this gift as a private attorney and as an attorney general, he fine-tuned it to high fidelity as a senator. One friend remembered how, when Frelinghuysen was excited about a speech, "His soul took fire. His logic was red hot. His appeals were irresistible. Before his audience were aware, they found themselves borne away at a master's will, and every thought and feeling absorbed in the rushing flow of the orator's voice." The same friend recalled in astonishment how words "tripped like nimble servitors at his bidding." Having spent many hours reading through the corpus of the senator's speeches, I can only give a sincere "amen" to these sentiments. Even today, his speeches communicate effectively, especially when read aloud. We can only imagine how powerful they would have sounded when delivered with Frelinghuysen's energy and style.

The oratorical style, however, was only one dimension of his communicative skills. Content and a Christian attitude toward content also stood out; in fact, it was the most important feature. Nowhere is this more apparent than in the following poignant quote from Tayler Lewis, later an educational colleague of Frelinghuysen:

> Here was something new in that Senate. Christianity had often been mentioned with approbation, but here was an exhibition of its very spirit and power. There was something in the tone of those speeches...which showed that religion was there in their midst—hearty, fervent, evangelical religion—religion as a higher law...instead of that mere political patronizing of Christianity which is so common among our public men....Mr. Frelinghuysen's soul was in these speeches. He was pleading for Christ, his Savior.

No better comment could be made of Frelinghuysen's Christian statesmanship than these words of Lewis. They pointed to the spiritual dimension of the senator's message, the very gospel itself. It was this dimension which he wanted to shine most brightly, just as it was this message which gave him comfort and hope personally.

Yet, this fairly popular Christian statesman remained apprehensive as the 1834 election approached. His defiance of the legislature, to be sure, was a source of uneasiness, but it was not the principal one; legislative opposition could be overcome by a strong showing at the polls by the newly-formed Whig party. But that was the rub. The National-Republicans (the Whigs) had lost control the previous year and appeared to be in trouble again in 1834. One cause particularly gave the Democrats confidence: the nearly unanimous support of a strong faction within the Society of Friends, namely the "Hicksites." This Quaker faction had supported the Democrats in the statewide 1833 elections, tipping the scales against Frelinghuysen's party. In 1834 all signs again pointed to a major Hicksite effort to deny victory to the Whigs. Why? And what role had Frelinghuysen played in this political-cultural drama?

Quakers, of course, had made many contributions to New Jersey's history. Both East Jersey and West Jersey had been formed by groups of proprietors of whom many were Quakers seeking religious freedom and a peaceful society. As colonial life unfolded, they grew numerous and prosperous, becoming a major cultural force in New Jersey. The "peaceable kingdom," however, was torn apart in the early 1800's by the appearance of a charismatic leader, Elias Hicks, who attracted to himself a sizeable portion of the state's Quakers. For the original, or orthodox Quakers, Hicks was dangerous because he preached a far different gospel than the one handed down to them by George Fox and his descendants. In fact, many orthodox Quakers considered Hicks a heretic.

The controversy between the two factions reached a crisis in 1827. At that time, both factions claimed to have authority to control the property of the Society of Friends, as such property had been bequeathed to them by previous generations. In particular dispute were the funds for educating needy Quaker children originally established in 1792. Who would control the distribution of this property? The subsequent legal action eventually reached the Chancery Court in 1832. After lengthy testimony, the lower court decided in favor of the orthodox Quakers. Hicksites were naturally upset and sought reversal on appeal in 1833.

Both sides brought out their legal big guns for the battle in the Court of Appeals. The Hicksites secured the services of Garret D. Wall and Samuel Southard, and the orthodox Quakers turned to George Wood and Theodore Frelinghuysen. The second trial was held in Trenton, the state capital, during July and August of 1833. New Jersey had not experienced such a controversial trial since the 1812 murder case involving the black man. "During most of the week," reported Trenton's *New Jersey Star Gazette* on August 10, "the town has been thronged with persons feeling an interest in the case, and others attracted by curiosity to hear the exposition of the cause by the able and learned counsel engaged in the controversy." Frelinghuysen's defense of the orthodox position took place in August and included three days of testimony. It was an eloquent presentation, worth summarizing in terms of its content and immediate repercussions.

In his defense of orthodox Quakers, Frelinghuysen quickly pointed out that much more was at stake than the "paltry" sum of $2,000, the amount of property in dispute. The real argument involved both the theological integrity of the Quakers and, more importantly, the very foundations of historic Christianity. Consequently, few disputes were as crucial for New Jersey or the nation as this one. Hicksites alleged that Quakers had no formal creed and therefore could follow their conscience in matters of theology and practice. Frelinghuysen showed the foolishness of this posture:

> This proposition of our adversaries, that there is no guide, nor leader, nor system of faith among them, would lead to dreadful consequences. It breaks up all order and authority; every man is to think as he pleases and, the step is a short one, to act as he pleases. It is downright radicalism; it would drive liberty, happiness, and religion away forever.

Far from holding such a preposterous position, Quakers were champions of order and decency, precisely because they had a definite creed, a creed that was to be found, according to Frelinghuysen, in the Bible. The literal words of Scripture functioned as a creed for the Society of Friends: "In what better clothing could they exhibit their faith....it seems to me, that the safest and clearest exhibition of a man's belief, may be expressed in Scripture language."

Commitment to the literal words of Scripture led Quakers to orthodox positions on key Biblical doctrines, especially the divinity of Christ, the blood atonement of the Cross, and the authority of Scripture itself. Frelinghuysen argued that Quakers had always held these "doctrines" and to attack them on these issues was to threaten historic Christianity. Elias Hicks posed such a threat, in his opinion.

The main burden of Frelinghuysen's testimony, therefore, was to reveal the true colors of secessionist leader Elias Hicks. In the strongest and boldest terms he exposed the "heretical doctrines" of Hicks, warning the court against the dangerous course of siding with this unstable figure. Hicks denied, said Frelinghuysen, the essential Christian doctrines of original sin, the divinity of Christ, the Trinity, the Virgin birth, and the bodily resurrection of the Savior. "He makes one fell swoop of the Bible," claimed the attorney, "tearing up the anchor of our hopes, and leaves us without a guide upon the ocean of speculation." It was merely consistent for Hicks to conclude that only a "dupe" would submit to the Bible and its literal teachings.

Frelinghuysen kept up his relentless attack on Hicks's position for several hours; in terms of the published accounts, it covered fourteen pages. All of Hicks's allegations were countered, point for point; no concessions appeared, no compromise made with Hicksite theology. All of the troubles experienced by the Quakers—the tragic secession and the dispute over property—were laid at the feet of Elias Hicks. "Spoiler'' was the role he had chosen to play, and he had played it to the bitter end.

Frelinghuysen ended his three days' testimony by calling on the Appeals Court to honor the ''sacred trust'' of the orthodox Quakers. The trust had been established to educate children in the doctrines of Scripture as believed by the original Society of Friends, not the usurpers. It must not be divided with heretics, the senator pleaded. The court, in the end, leaned markedly in his direction and voted to uphold the lower court decision; the orthodox Quakers were once again victorious.

But it was a Pyrrhic victory for Frelinghuysen. His masterly, and appropriate, defense of orthodox Christianity proved to be his political undoing. The Hicksites unleashed their fury at everyone associated with their humiliation and defeat. For example, Justice Drake, the original presiding judge, felt the heat of their anger; he was replaced shortly after the 1833 decision. The National-Republicans also went down to defeat in 1833, thanks to the block voting of the Hicksite faction. But Frelinghuysen was the primary target of their ''righteous'' wrath. As 1834 unfolded, it became obvious that animosity lingered; Hicksites were determined to unseat him by voting Democratic and subsequently denying him a second term via reappointment. They lobbied heavily against him throughout the state. Frelinghuysen and the Whigs attempted to win back some support, but they were not overly optimistic on the eve of the election. The Hicksite hostility posed a serious problem in a state fairly evenly divided between two political parties.

Frelinghuysen's fears were well founded. The Democrats carried the state again, with Hicksite support the key factor. In a letter to a friend, Tristram Burges, on October 18, 1834, Frelinghuysen acknowledged the role Hicksite opposition played in his defeat. Whigs had regained some of the support lost in 1833, but not enough to change the overall outcome. The inevitable then quickly occurred: Garret Wall, the Hicksite lawyer, was rewarded for his efforts by being selected to replace Frelinghuysen in 1835. The Christian statesman's Senate career was over. What would happen to him now? Would this also be the end of his political service and his public ministry?

* * * * * * *

Discussion Questions

1. Under what circumstances should a Christian politician claim to know the will of the people? Should this ever be done in defiance of another group of elected officials? Under what circumstances? What are the dangers in staking out such a position?

2. How important are concrete legislative results for a Christian politician? Are other considerations more important than legislative suc-

cess? Name some. Name a politician who is "successful" in ways other than the practical-legislative. What draws you to him/her?

3. I suggested that Frelinghuysen displayed independence as a senator. How important is this attribute? Should a Christian politician be more loyal to conscience or his party's platform and position? If your answer is conscience, then what role do parties play in American politics?

4. Frelinghuysen was noted for cordial interpersonal relationships as a senator. How important is this trait for effectiveness? In other words, does cordiality enhance political effectiveness? Why or why not?

5. Frelinghuysen was a great orator. In terms of our contemporary politics, how important is the art of public speaking and persuasion? How much should a contemporary Christian politician rely on public relations and the media? Name a Christian politician who uses them effectively. What abuses are potentially present in relying on these modern phenomena?

6. What moral lessons would you draw from Frelinghuysen's defense of the orthodox Quakers in the Quaker Case of 1833? Can you think of any modern parallels to this case?

7. From a political point of view, would it have been better for Frelinghuysen to avoid the Quaker case? In other words, was it politically wise, in light of the historical context? (Should Christians avoid controversy to enhance their chances for reelection?)

Chapter 5

5,106

> There is not a man of purer character, of more sober temperament, of more accessible manners, and of more firm, unbending, uncompromising Whig principles than Theodore Frelinghuysen; and not only is he all this, but such is the ease of his manners, such the spotless purity of his life, such the sterling attributes of his character, that he has the regard, the fervent attachment, and the enduring love of all who know him.
>
> —Daniel Webster, 1844

> It is cynical for the Whigs to place "the Christian statesman" on the same ticket as the "reprobate" Henry Clay.
>
> —Lewis Tappan, 1844

Everyone waited uneasily as the early days of November, 1844, rolled by. The presidential election had been concluded, but slow communications and slower tabulation of results kept the suspense alive, day after day. It was obvious from early returns that it was going to be a cliff-hanger. Experts had predicted the swing state to be New York; whichever way New York tipped, so would the nation. Henry Clay waited nervously for the final results. At the age of sixty-seven, running for the third time, he suspected it was his last chance.

Theodore Frelinghuysen, Clay's vice-presidential running mate, also waited, but with a far different attitude. Although fairly confident of victory, he approached the countdown with equanimity. Because of a deep faith in God and a sense of purpose, he faced the future confidently, whatever the outcome. Service to God would not end with failure to secure the vice-presidency.

By mid-November the final returns were in, and the experts were proved right; New York was the key, falling by 5,106 votes to the Democratic ticket of James Polk and George Dallas. Had the Empire State gone the other way, the aging Clay would have finally achieved his ultimate prize—and Theodore Frelinghuysen would have been a heartbeat away from the presidency. Naturally, the two Whig candidates responded in different ways to the outcome; in fact, Frelinghuysen accepted his fate with the "pious cheerfulness that could have been only a little short of irritating to the stunned and embittered Clay." Despondency and cheerful serenity, two quite contrasting responses from two contrasting personalities.

It had taken time, however, for Frelinghuysen to achieve emotional maturity. His immediate response to his own political misfortunes in 1834-35 had not been so calm. Losing the Senate seat disappointed him; he had enjoyed the visibility and excitement of Washington as well as the opportunity to serve his God politically. Perhaps, he pondered, the loss was a sign from God to shift the focus of his life? Perhaps God was calling him to the "ministry proper," i.e., to the pastorate?

Such thinking is understandable in light of Frelinghuysen's evangelical environment and commitment. And he had plenty of company; many evangelical young men wondered (as they do today) whether or not they should use their talents in "full-time ministry." That phrase meant pastoring a church or becoming a missionary. Thus, in 1835, the fork in the road for Frelinghuysen meant politics and nonchurch service on the one hand, or the pulpit or a church-related ministry on the other.

The dilemma was a bothersome one. For a time, he apparently leaned in the direction of the pastorate, though it would require advanced seminary training. But, forty-eight years old, he was willing to make the sacrifice if it pleased God. During these crucial months, however, a friend appeared with a different message. His name was Gardiner Spring, and he knew what Frelinghuysen was going through. He too had begun as a lawyer, but he had changed vocations, opting for the pulpit rather than the bar. It was natural, then, for Frelinghuysen to seek his advice at this critical time. They talked and corresponded until a decision was reached: Frelinghuysen would be a lawyer, a politician, a public servant, rather than a pastor. He had no convincing argument with the insightful summary of the dilemma as presented by Spring:

> Your present influence and standing at the bar and in civil life are against the change. Influence and character are plants of slow growth... I have my doubts whether you can do as much for the cause of the blessed Redeemer in the ministry of reconciliation as you now do in your present and kindred relations. Our Master needs laborers in Church and State. Such is the feeling and such are the institutions of this country that ministers of the Gospel can get very little influence on the state, and therefore, there is the more need for men who are qualified and have the spirit of ministers to retain their political influence.

God had brought Rev. Spring into his life at the right moment. His testimony and Frelinghuysen's Reformed-Calvinistic roots combined to end the wavering. He was at peace in late 1835, ready to follow where God would lead him in the arena of public life.

Frelinghuysen first felt led back into law, returning to an important and lucrative practice. Being an attorney allowed him to maintain political contacts and keep his finger on the pulse of the state. As a lawyer, he also had time to provide some leadership for the fledgling Whig party organization in New Jersey. The nitty-gritty political work wasn't glamorous, but it needed to be done. He served willingly.

The first tangible reward for his faithful service to the cause of Whiggery occurred in 1837, when Newark, New Jersey, needed executive leadership. New York's growing and potentially prosperous neighbor had just been incorporated in 1836. The following spring, an election was held for the first mayoralty, and Frelinghuysen triumphed, beginning the first of his two one-year terms as Newark's chief executive.

The former legislator did a commendable job as Newark's mayor. It was no easy task. Not only was the office a new one, but the city had just entered the bleak world being created by the Panic of 1837. Because of this recession, Newark faced a desperate financial situation; revenues had dried up, coffers were empty, and the people "clamored for relief." Frelinghuysen faced the complex situation with both fiscal responsibility and compassion.

His conservative fiscal restraint can be seen operating in several areas. For example, Frelinghuysen vetoed a resolution of the Common Council calling for a new water project because he felt it added too much to the public debt. For a similar reason, he opposed the Council's efforts to build a major new canal on the Passaic River. He also approved of a measure, later adopted, directed against the "growing evils of incendiaries," i.e., urban mobs driven to extremes by economic despair. Finally, he implored New Jersey and New York City authorities to deal with the problems associated with the influx of substantial numbers of immigrants into the metropolitan area. Many were poor and ended up on Newark's doorstep, causing "great consternation" in the city. His particular response to the potentially tragic situation came in the form of a request requiring masters of vessels to be liable financially for the immigrants, thus retarding the drain on Newark's resources.

But fiscal conservatism only tells part of the story. Indications, paradoxically, of a more "liberal" attitude also surfaced during the mayor's two terms, consistent with what I previously called "compassionate statism." Even two of the above examples of conservatism had that "liberal" dimension to them: after vetoing the Council's bid to construct a new water project, he turned around and approved legislation to grant expenditures for other means of receiving water; and he softened his objection to a new canal by approving expenditures to enhance existing navigation in the area of Newark Bay. The best example, however, of his compassionate statism came in the area of education. Frelinghuysen pushed successfully for the establishment of new district schools in Newark and fought especially hard for additional appropriations for the education of the poor and the disadvantaged, e.g., the Colored School and a school for orphans. In so doing, he resisted the strong movement toward absolute fiscal restraint in Newark. Education, it seems, was too important to him for it to be slashed, even during a period of economic stagnation.

A third feature of his mayoralty resembles what I have called "Christian confessionalism," consistent, once again, with the principles he held to throughout his public life. Ever conscious of the duty of the state to acknowledge its dependence on God and submit to His creation order, he supported efforts to prohibit railroads and canal companies from conducting normal business on Sunday. Success in the form of appropriate legislation modified slightly by the Common Council rewarded his efforts on both fronts.

In short, Frelinghuysen's years as mayor were successful, appropriately blending elements of fiscal restraint and compassionate spending in an overall context of confessional Christianity. He proved to be neither dogmatically conservative nor dogmatically liberal but instead a politician who could transcend both slippery labels. Drawing upon his experience as a legislator in Washington and his developing faith, he assumed to a noticeable degree the posture of a Christian "executive," a mayor who exercised his office normatively. It's a shame that he didn't have more time in Newark to sharpen his skills.

His final opportunity for political service occurred in 1844 as the Whig's nominee for vice-president. By this time, Frelinghuysen had provided five years of educational leadership as the chancellor of New York University. That he had felt led away from politics in 1839 should not be seen as an abandonment of public service but rather as a shifting of focus from one kind of public ministry to another. Today's distinction between public arenas and private institutions hardly held for antebellum America: being chancellor of N.Y.U. was public service of the highest order! Still, it wasn't political service as such, and Frelinghuysen hadn't rid himself entirely of the political virus. Allowing his name to be offered for serious consideration for the vice-presidential nomination was—for the fifty-seven year old educator—the last deliberate fling of his hat into the political ring.

The Whig party met in convention at Baltimore in April and May, 1844. There was little doubt that Clay would be nominated for president. The Whigs sought not only to retain the presidency but to return the party to its true ideological roots; they felt betrayed by President John Tyler, who had assumed the highest office upon the death of William Harrison in 1841. Tyler had lost the support of the Whig congressional leaders by challenging them on several key issues, including banking and slavery. In their opinion, he was not fit to be considered an incumbent and therefore be automatically renominated. Lacking any substantial support, Tyler withdrew his name from consideration before the start of the convention. Clay arrived in Baltimore a virtual shoo-in for the nomination.

As the overwhelming favorite, Clay turned the convention into a "love feast" for himself and his version of Whiggery. The resulting Whig platform called for a "well-regulated currency," a wise and efficient government, a moderately high tariff to defray government expenses, protection of domestic labor (and by implication American industry), opposition to executive usurpations (by Democrats and by implication fellow-travelers like Tyler), and a single-term presidency. The document being a concise and clear expression of Clay's own American system, no doubt he was pleased to run on it.

The only glaring omission was a lack of any reference to the slavery issue: the issues related to the expansion of slavery into new territories in conflict with the tenets of abolitionism were not allowed to threaten the cautious master plan designed to grab the White House for the Kentuckian. But in a nation where slavery was already emerging as the number one subject, such hesitancy was almost as dangerous as taking sides on the issue.

The only substantial issue to be resolved at the convention was the selection of a vice-presidential nominee. The leading candidates were John Sergeant of Pennsylvania, John Davis of Massachusetts, Millard Fillmore of New York (later to become president), and Theodore Frelinghuysen. Clay, apparently as a gesture of unity, allowed the convention to select a candidate for the second position. On the third ballot the majority voted for New Jersey's favorite son.

Why Frelinghuysen? The answer, I believe, has several dimensions. First, he was a recognized and respected national leader, one who had "such experience in public affairs and acquaintance with public men," said William Hunt in 1938, "[that he had] a national reputation whose extent is difficult to appreciate [in the twentieth century]." Second, he was not only a national leader in a general sense, but also the preeminent Christian leader, an outspoken evangelical in a still largely evangelical Protestant country. According to *The Sunday Call* (Newark), Frelinghuysen "was by no means the mere figurehead that some Vice Presidential candidates have been, but, on the contrary, added great strength to the Whig ticket." In other words, his name was recognized in both worlds, the Christian as well as the secular.

A third factor dealt with the contrasting personalities and life styles of the two nominees. Henry Clay had long been known as a "worldly" man. Throughout most of his life, he was a heavy drinker who also freely indulged his passion for gambling. Further, he had fought several famous duels as a young man and could thereafter never fully escape his reputation for violence and vendetta. Although hardly a reprobate in 1844, his name was sufficiently soiled to lead the convention to select someone with opposite qualities, hoping therefore to add a meas-

41

ure of respectability to the campaign. In short, Frelinghuysen was chosen because of his "saintly" reputation. Here was a man who abstained from drink and gambling, abhorred the very thought of dueling, and even resisted the Whig managers who tried to "dance Harry into the White House," the waltz having become the new rage in high society.

Finally, the candidates' differing geographical affiliations need to be noted. The Whig strategy in 1844—like today's campaigns—utilized a geo-political balancing principle. Clay's appeal lay mostly with the West and, the party hoped, the South. The key missing piece to the electoral puzzle was the Northeast. Without New York and Pennsylvania, Clay's chances were remote at best. What better ploy for Clay's managers than to exploit Frelinghuysen as a dignified Christian statesman with roots deeply planted in the industrial Northeast.

All these reasons combined with his natural friendliness and warmth, made the university chancellor the ideal counterpart to Henry Clay. In Hunt's words, "The selection of Frelinghuysen had every appearance of being a complete fulfillment of all the necessities in a [vice-presidential] candidate." The juxtaposition was paradoxically appropriate: saint and sinner, East and West; "The nation's rising for Clay and Frelinghuysen," sang the jubilant Whigs!

High emotional involvement characterized both major parties in the 1844 campaign. The Democrats were just as determined to regain the presidency as were the Whigs to retain and purify it. Emotions intensified as charges and countercharges were hurled back and forth between the two camps. The Democrats, however, seemed to take the upper hand, as their frontal assault upon the Whigs proved to be more effective as a propaganda tool than did the nearly hysterical efforts by the Whigs to replay the Harrison triumph of 1840. Two points in particular stand out in their unremitting attack.

The slavery issue, or more precisely, the possibility of national expansion through the annexation of Texas as a proslavery state, surfaced immediately as a point of contention. Polk had seized the initiative on the issue by immediately declaring his support of annexation, even if it meant adding another slave state to the Union. This bold gambit put Clay on the defensive; his hope of avoiding the issue entirely was thus shattered at the outset of the campaign. Worse than opposing annexation outright, Clay seemed to waver, to drift back and forth—first denouncing annexation, then seeming to accept it but only under certain conditions. Each time he spoke the water became muddier.

Clay's waffling gave the Democrats plenty of ammunition. Driven by the erupting force of manifest destiny, they accused the Whig leader of failing to understand our true imperial future as a nation, one of inexorable expansion from the Atlantic to the Pacific. In effect, Clay's lack of nationalistic faith was "un-American." The Kentuckian's indecision also encouraged antislavery partisans. The Liberty party—a strident abolitionist third party, which was particularly strong in New York state—revived. This constellation of political antagonists produced an ironic result: the anti-Texas party, by swinging New York to Polk, actually hastened annexation (and the Civil War)!

Frelinghuysen could do little about the issue of annexation as such; the mess was of Clay's making. The number two man, however, was not forgotten by the Democrats: his reputation became the second focus of concentrated assault. The attack took two contradictory forms. On the one hand, Democrats joined some evangelicals, like Lewis Tappan, in questioning the propriety of matching saint with sinner. On the other hand, they unleashed a smear campaign *against* Frelinghuysen's Protestant evangelicalism, a campaign of "conscienceless ferocity," in the words of one historian. Their libel was directed primarily at the key states of Pennsylvania and New York whose principal cities were sheltering tens of thousands of new immigrants, mostly poor and mostly Catholic. Such cities, they believed, would be fertile ground for the seeds of religious bigotry. To nurture such prejudice, actually "to inflame the foreign-born vote and turn it to their purposes," the Polk managers criticized many of Frelinghuysen's religious connections, especially his leadership of missionary societies, the American Tract Society and the American Bible Society. Frelinghuysen and the benevolent associations were pictured as a threat to what the Catholic immigrants held dear. As one Democratic politician concluded in a more serene mood, "Mr. Frelinghuysen will never do [as a vice-president]; he's much too mixed up with these Bible societies."

No evidence exists of any anti-Catholicism or nativism on Frelinghuysen's part in this election; it was a creature only of propaganda. In fact, he went out of his way to avoid any appearance of bias. When confronted, for example, by reports of anti-Catholic violence in the Northeast involving attacks on Catholic schools and convents, he declared:

> I have never spoken but in decided condemnation of the mob scenes of violence and blood in Philadelphia, and have nothing to do with the matter of the division of the school funds between Catholics and Protestants in New York....Allow me to say...that I cherish the principles of our Constitution, which allow full freedom of conscience and so forbid all religious [discrimination].

Despite these denials, nonetheless, the campaign of libel and slander against Frelinghuysen no doubt helped to swing immigrants' votes away from the Whigs, assuring a Democratic victory.

When looking at the 1844 campaign, we need to highlight a final incongruity, namely, the surprisingly small role played by Frelinghuysen in the actual electioneering. Why was a recognized leader like Frelinghuysen relegated to the back seat? Partly, I think, this was the natural role assigned to vice-presidential candidates, a role which has generally been true down to the present day. Whigs may have been singing about rising to Clay and Frelinghuysen, but the "songster" published for the campaign made it clear that Harry was the star of the show. Far more of the trite tunes and lyrics were devoted to Clay than to his running mate. Apparently, the Whigs were afraid that Chancellor Frelinghuysen might steal the spotlight from their aging warrior, a not unreasonable fear in light of the quality of his partner.

Another reason is related to the nature of his job as chancellor of a prestigious educational institution like New York University. His job was time-consuming and emotionally demanding. He believed that his first priority rested with his university and consequently chose to limit his campaign appearances to a few brief functions held close to New York City. A few critics have faulted him for this decision, especially in light of his renowned oratorical gifts. They have a point. Perhaps he could have changed the outcome in this close election. But it was not to be; he made his decision early and stuck with it.

I'm inclined to think, however, that the principal reason for Frelinghuysen's inaction was a personal one, i.e., a clash of contrasting lifestyles, attitudes, and commitments between himself and the party leader. There was a certain degree of underlying tension between the two standard-bearers, an uneasiness, even awkwardness, involving life's fundamental questions. To be sure, everything was fine on the surface. Frelinghuysen praised Clay and was complimented in return: "Nothing could be more agreeable and gratifying to me," declared Clay, "than the association of Mr. Frelinghuysen's name with my own....no man stands higher in my estimation as a pure, upright, and patriotic citizen." Yet, the two politicians were not close, not cronies; Frelinghuysen was never a part of the "inner circle." There was a "spiritual battle" going on between the two men, one which created and perpetuated the estrangement between them. A future chapter will bring that dilemma into sharper focus.

"There is not a man...of more firm, unbending, uncompromising Whig principles than Theodore Frelinghuysen," declared Daniel Webster on the eve of the 1844 campaign. How sad then that the natural philosophical alliance between the running mates could not be developed to the fullest. But we can say even more about the chancellor's commitment to a Whig America. For him, Whig principles had always been close to Christian principles. Far more important than electoral success had been the task of articulating these tenets so indispensable to liberty and democracy. That he paused in the late 1830's to publish his principles in book form should come as no surprise.

* * * * * * *

44

Discussion Questions

1. After losing his Senate seat, Frelinghuysen considered leaving politics altogether for "full-time" Christian service. What is the danger in setting up this dichotomy? Is there a sense in which politics can be seen as "full-time" service?

2. I suggested that as mayor of Newark Frelinghuysen managed to transcend the labels of "liberal" and "conservative." To what extent do you feel it is possible today for a Christian politician to avoid these labels? What would you call such a politician?

3. Is it possible that Frelinghuysen was being "exploited" by Henry Clay, i.e., used somewhat cynically for his evangelical connections? Can you think of Christian political leaders today who are being manipulated by others for unsavory or selfish purposes? What attitude should we take to such manipulation? How could it be avoided?

4. Frelinghuysen was attacked viciously by his opponents in the 1844 campaign, being accused of anti-Catholicism and hatred of immigrants. How should Christian leaders respond to slander and libel? In politics is there ever a time to respond in kind, or should Christians always "turn the other cheek"?

5. What kind of vice-president or president do you think Frelinghuysen would have made? What would have been his strengths and weaknesses? Of today's Christian leaders, which one would make a good president? Why?

6. Can you think of any reasons today why Christians should not seek a high elective office such as vice-president or president? Name some.

7. On the basis of this chapter, why do you think there was tension between Clay and Frelinghuysen?

Chapter 6

A Whig America, A Christian America?

> We began as a Christian people...[and we are] not yet desper-
> ately fallen: Christianity is still incorporated with the frame
> of our government and laws: our intelligence, our virtue,
> our political freedom, still confess the impulse and enjoy the
> life it has given....
> —Theodore Frelinghuysen, 1838

> Government is a means, not an end; its use is to preserve
> peace, order, justice, among men....
> —Theodore Frelinghuysen, 1838

> Whig political culture was profoundly influenced by the Sec-
> ond Great Awakening, an outburst of evangelical activity
> which...sought to transform society along moral lines....[It]
> was not enough to win individual souls to Christ; society
> as a whole must respond to His call.
> —Daniel Walker Howe, 1979

Frelinghuysen's book, *An Inquiry into the Moral and Religious Character of the American Government,* was published by Wiley and Putnam
of New York City in 1838. It was a jeremiad of unusual power and
frankness, a clarion call for evangelicals and Reformed Christians to
awake from their spiritual lethargy and prepare for battle or risk losing
the soul of America itself to the forces of "irreligion."

Chapter one set the stage for his argument. Frelinghuysen minced
no words when he pointed the accusing finger at Thomas Jefferson and
Andrew Jackson. It was their political tradition in general and these men
in particular who were to blame for many of the national ills. They had
initiated a style of leadership which attempted to "[carry] on the business of the commonwealth *professedly* as 'without God in the world.' "
This misleadership, warned Newark's mayor, had natural consequences:
the seeds of irreligion which it helped to plant were now sprouting into
choking weeds threatening the life of the young republic.

Jefferson and Jackson were not the only culprits. Congress, too, must
share the blame for the country's misfortunes. The overall situation in

Congress was a "scandal"; many politicians were "demagogues," mere "partymen," coaxing citizens down the path of godlessness. For proof Frelinghuysen returned to the turmoil surrounding the Sunday mail controversy in the early 1830's. This sad tale had shown the true weakness of national leadership in America.

No level of government nor the citizenry itself was free from the debilitating effects of irreligion. Enlightened voting, for example, had suffered a severe blow:

> Has it not become a cant among us, that *as electors* we have
> nothing to do with men's religious sentiments; no right even
> to inquire about them? In a word, religion, even with those
> who make profession of it, is *nothing at an election.*

In sum, the religion which had made America great, lamented Frelinghuysen in the opening chapter, "is everywhere *politically set at nought,* regarded as an outlaw to the institutions of the country...as useless...in public life."

Several other developments had contributed to Frelinghuysen's uneasiness in 1838. First, the Panic of 1837 was causing a severe drain on the finances of many of the organizations which made up the "benevolent empire." Within months many of these organizations had been forced to cut budgets and reduce their various ministries. How, Frelinghuysen wondered, could irreligion be fought if Christians' weapons were taken away from them? Second, we have seen how much he was disturbed by the rapidly increasing tide of immigrants washing onto the shores of greater New York. By the late 1830's, this tide was less Protestant and Anglo-Saxon than previously, causing the mayor to wonder about the constituency of America's religious future. Third, Protestant unity itself was in question during these years. Some denominations had begun withdrawing their support of the benevolent empire; others were breaking apart internally. The Presbyterian Church, for example, was splitting into "Old School" and "New School" factions at this time. Frelinghuysen had devoted much of his time and effort to the Presbyterian Church in his early adult years and found the rupture difficult to accept emotionally. These three developments—stemming from the irreligion rampant in America—were more than sufficient reason for alarm in Frelinghuysen's mind.

Reformation was the need of the hour, a re-formation of the American experiment. And who, I can imagine him wondering, was better able to point out the need for reformation than himself? Had he not been leading the fight for morality in government for much of his life? With that kind of political experience, who was better prepared to defend the moral-religious foundation of American government and warn of departure from it than Mayor Frelinghuysen?

Before examining the remaining eight chapters of the book, I want to put the narrative into contemporary focus, juxtaposing it with some of the church-state issues that are relevant to our own generation. Contemporary scholars, when referring to Frelinghuysen's approach to government, criticize him for "blatant" attempts to impose a narrow religious perspective on a (supposedly) neutral, secular political arena. Arthur Schlesinger, Jr., for example, claims that Frelinghuysen was America's leading advocate for "the re-establishment of the belief in the religious character of the state and, thus, in the supremacy of religious interests [in politics]." John Bodo and others come to similar conclusions about the apparent theocratic tendencies deeply ingrained in the minds of Frelinghuysen and other champions of the benevolent empire.

How valid are these allegations, especially when directed at Frelinghuysen? Was he a theocrat? Did he believe in a "Christian" America? If so, to what extent, and what evidence is there that he believed in such a theocracy? If it wasn't exactly a Christian America he wanted, then what kind of America was it? These questions concerning Frelinghuysen are particularly relevant today because of the recent flood of literature from evangelical scholars devoted to similar topics. It appears that a progressive-conservative struggle is going on among evangelical scholars in an effort to determine the "truth" about America's religious history. It is an intellectually stimulating debate which the progressives seem to be winning, at least among mainstream evangelicalism. Thus, a consensus is emerging among our leading historians and scholars that America was never really a Christian nation; all attempts to prove the opposite are pathetically misguided. I assume, therefore, that, if these scholars would read his book, their response to the jeremiad would be largely a negative one, seeing it as an example of Frelinghuysen's poor reading of history and of his misplaced loyalty, his misguided nationalism. Whether this is an appropriate assessment can perhaps be determined by a careful reading of the rest of the book.

The Constitution itself was the subject of Frelinghuysen's second chapter. "Is the Constitution unfriendly to religion?" he asked at the outset. "No!" came his resounding answer. He acknowledged that the two constitutional provisions enumerated in the first amendment were stated in negative terms but quickly added that this proved very little. Besides, religion—true religion—did not need government support, he declared. In fact, it "thrives" when left alone.

The question concerning theocracy thus is easy to answer on the basis of this chapter: he rejected it outright. All attempts at religious "tests" for voting or holding office and all efforts at the establishment of religion were wrong and should be denounced whenever proposed. He even argued that such unwise combinations of church and state came not from sincere Christians but from the secular world and "nominal" Christians. No Christian who understood his faith would ever accept the "bribe" implicit in church-state entanglements. Today's progressive evangelical scholars would no doubt breathe a sigh of relief when finishing the second chapter.

The question involving commitment to a Christian nation, however, is another matter. Here the material—as garnered from chapters three through nine—seems to point strongly toward the affirmative, i.e., that Frelinghuysen did believe in America as a Christian nation. Yet even this, I will show after the summary of the chapters, can be interpreted in a positive manner, one avoiding an extreme form of religious American nationalism.

Chapter three dealt with colonial history. In the colonial context the Christian lawyer found his greatest case for "presumptive evidence" regarding the Constitution, historical evidence which would undermine the "argument from silence" used by his irreligious opponents in their interpretation of the Constitution. In other words, if he could show the pervasive influence of Christianity throughout colonial political life, he could conclude that the founding fathers "presumed" the new nation to be essentially Christian. And everywhere he looked he found abundant evidence!

The Christianity of colonial New England, he asserted, was apparent to all: "[In New England] religion itself, the great principle of the fear and love of God, was at the bottom of all, the abiding basis on which every public measure was founded, every legal and even political structure reared." Almost all the other colonies had similar histories: Pennsylvania was "eminently a Christian colony,...[where] Christianity was the religion of the laws." New Jersey was a "Christian community, sound in the ingredients of [its] composition." Virginia had a strong "tide of religious feeling [running] among the people." In short, the colonies were pervasively religious:

> Whatever may have happened more recently, there was a
> time when Christian piety, instead of being under public re-
> proach, was popular, was general, was nearly universal in
> the country; respected by all men, and by most regarded as
> the best of earthly possessions. We are descended, God be
> thanked, from Christian parents. Religion was the fountain-
> head of our liberty.

In chapter four Frelinghuysen's sharp lawyer's eye perused the various state constitutions adopted during the Revolutionary period. Once again, he found ample evidence of a national commitment to Christianity. Of the thirteen original state constitutions, only three—Virginia's, Connecticut's, and Rhode Island's—made no mention of God or (the Christian) religion. Of the ten which did, he showed by a judicious use of quotes, most were explicitly "pro-religion."

Extensive quotations from state constitutions were crucial because of

Frelinghuysen's continuing concern to justify the lack of positive reference to God and religion in the federal Constitution. Logically, he reiterated, the promotion of religion in the state documents was tantamount to a similar positive bias in the federal document, since federal and state constitutions were "closely related." He concluded:

> Consistent with themselves, the people of 1787 meant by the federal arrangement nothing but a new and larger organization of government on principles already familiar to them....Does [the Constitution] proclaim itself unChristian? For if it's merely silent in the matter, law and reason both tell us that its religious character is to be looked for by interpretation, among the people that fashioned it; a people, Christian by profession and by genealogy....

"The Present Character of the State Systems" was the title of the fifth chapter. In it the Christian statesman showed how—despite the rise of irreligion—the positive laws of the various states remained essentially Christian. For evidence of "Christian laws" he cited numerous statutes which honored the Sabbath, prohibited profane language, and protected the special status of the clergy (e.g., laws forbidding the arrest of clergy while they were on official business). These and many other statutes all were "a pretty sure index of the prevailing popular sense of the country on that subject [of religion]."

It is understandable then that he found an even more persuasive case for the prevalence of Christianity in America's "common law" tradition. Common law, even more than positive law, was thoroughly Christian. For proof he cited a contemporary case of blasphemy heard in a Pennsylvania court. That the accused was guilty did not surprise him since, as he approvingly quoted the presiding judge, "Christianity, general Christianity, was and always has been a part of the common law of Pennsylvania."

> If these things are so [he summed up the chapter] then...the structure of the republic [is] still radically Christian....[We have adopted] the great outlines of [Christian] doctrine, cherishing its very forms, resting upon it, and making it to our jurisprudence what its author is to our faith, the rock of ages....

In chapter six Frelinghuysen turned his attention to the historical practice of the federal government regarding religion. A similar picture emerged: the three branches of government incarnated Christian themes. The national legislature opened its sessions with prayer and called upon citizens to engage in appropriate prayer and fasting, supported its own chaplains, and developed a military code which upheld the ethical basis of the Christian religion. The executive—despite the derelictions of Jefferson and Jackson—had generally been "direct and honest" in its diplomacy and benevolent in times of national disaster. Finally, the judiciary was even more integrally Christian: as a common law tribunal it guarded public morals by caring for needy children, insisting on Christian burials, adjudicating against public drunkenness and nakedness, and, most importantly, requiring a "Bible oath" for legal testimony. As a nation we could be rightfully proud of our historic federal policy:

> The impartiality...of our laws is theoretically perfect....We have not only no preference of Christian sects, but none of ranks...and none of individual pretenders....[Our] poor are cared for: everything takes the place which on Christian principles belong to it. How marvelous that such a government should have incurred the reproach of being unchristian, or even indifferent to Christianity.

Even if for no deeper reason, accepting Christianity merely because it was expedient could lead to valuable results for Americans. In chapter seven Frelinghuysen argued that it was the height of wisdom to obey the Bible even if it *may be* true. Why? Because only a fool would fail to recognize that Christianity led directly to (1) civilization, (2) moral elevation of all people, and (3) opposition to political tyranny. And expediency was the path of wisdom for nations and states as well as for individuals, since nations too were moral beings accountable for their actions. Obedience led to national blessing and prosperity, he thankfully concluded. If for no other reason, Christianity ought to be chosen just on this basis.

In chapter eight Frelinghuysen briefly assumed the mantle of political philosopher. Why, he queried, were there so many popular misconceptions about religion in American life? Why so much confusion over issues like Sunday mail? The answer was simple: Americans had forgotten the distinction between two types of Christianity: "ecclesiastical" and "ethical." Ecclesiastical Christianity dealt with the institutional church, with sects, whereas ethical Christianity was the general framework acceptable to all believers. He summarized it in these words:

> Ecclesiastical Christianity is neither to be adopted nor rejected by political men as such. Honour it, and let it alone. Regard it not as evil, but rather as an infinite good, which yet may become evil by abuse. Ethical Christianity, however, should be embraced, as well as honoured. Our statesmen, our administrators, cannot possibly have too much of it.

The trouble with the irreligious, he reminded his readers, was their desire to avoid both expressions of Christianity. But the latter—ethical Christianity—was the "animating principle" of our government. Without it we would perish. "Is nothing to be considered at rest in the political world?" he warned. "Are first principles...to be tossed and sported with in endless agitation...?"

"No," he answered in the final chapter. Americans must be committed to these "first principles," and these principles implied action. Minimally, we should stop railing against religion in public life and expect a positive ethical example from our leaders. But much more was needed: "The very springs of our political action should be readjusted....We want...more than honesty, we want government honestly administered on Christian principles and with Christian ends in view...." In other words, *reformation* was necessary, a deep, Biblical reformation.

What conclusions about the style as well as the direction of his argument can we draw from the bulk of Frelinghuysen's book? Several stand out. First, his style of argumentation is impressive, although it is perhaps a little too forensic, a little too neatly wrapped for our own tastes. Frelinghuysen, the lawyer, occasionally got carried away with his own logic. Second, his marshalling of "evidence" is also impressive but perhaps too much of a good thing. Reading his book we are confronted with many long-forgotten historical details, each of them interesting in its own right. I believe though that the sheer bulk of the details is too overwhelming, almost too patently an attempt to be convincing. He avoided presenting and directly dealing with the counter-evidence. Third, Frelinghuysen's promotion of America as a Christian nation is obvious even to the casual reader. But we must still ask what this means. Does it mean—as perhaps some evangelicals would argue—that Frelinghuysen was engaged in the worst features of extreme Christian nationalism, where America, as much as the God of Scriptures, becomes the object of worship, where our system of government is seen as Biblical *per se?* I hardly think so.

In the book Frelinghuysen alerted readers to the "democratic tyranny" implicit in their political system and its rulers. Only the Bible could save them, only it

> sets the glories of earthly potentates before us in their true
> dimensions; stripping them of their enchantment; putting
> down their high looks and imaginations; causing us to see
> that man in office is still man...that pride is [an] abomina-
> tion....and that all flesh, however clothed...is grass.

"We are too proud of our liberties and our blessings," he warned in another context. "Self-confidence is engendered, [as well as] a spirit of individual independence almost too strong for law." No political system including the American one was perfect nor should it be bathed in the light of universal Christian approbation.

He also frequently pointed out the positive features of other nations and their political systems. England especially received his nod of approval, as did Scotland and Holland—a place of "enlightened freedom." America was not the only example of political democracy, not the only model an "unenlightened" world could follow. American democracy could not and should not be presented as an absolute among political systems.

What then was America's most important task? Clearly, not to champion *its own system,* but to help lead "the family of nations from all her rebellions, back to their rightful sovereign." America could not *be* God; it had to point the way *to* God!

Whiggery

Frelinghuysen was no pluralist in the sense that many evangelicals and Reformed Christians would use the term today. His inability to "tolerate" the political expression of irreligion would not match up to our own broader tolerance. Yet his perspective was not excessive, especially for his time. In fact, most of his views were in the political mainstream of antebellum America. That is why I prefer to change the image and to label his vision as one of a Whig America rather than of a Christian America. Whiggery was his actual program, not the apocalyptic politics implied in his rhetoric. Religion, of course, was an important feature of antebellum Whiggery. The Second Great Awakening in particular helped to pave the way for a developing Whig culture. But "religion" paints only part of the picture, both for the Whigs and, I'm arguing, for Frelinghuysen as well.

I have found one treatment of the Whigs especially helpful for painting the total picture: Daniel Walker Howe's *The Political Culture of American Whigs* (1979). The varied causes and aspects of Whiggery have never been so masterfully analyzed. From Howe's account we learn that Whigs were committed to all of the following principles or programs: national development through a "positive liberal state" (he has chapters on Henry Clay and Daniel Webster); a creative combination of capitalistic progress and social paternalism; an orderly society, yet one where social reform is possible through voluntary associations (Lyman Beecher is his choice as a leader of the benevolent empire); distrust of executive power; redemption of America through education; constitutionalism; and belief in technology as one key to the future. Howe also stresses the great oratorical skills which were used by Protestant leaders to issue didactic moral appeals. Combined, these principles and attributes spell out a political system clearly distinguishable from that of the Democratic party. Some overlapped, of course, such as constitutionalism and oratorical skills, but most were unique to American Whigs.

As I indicated above, Howe finds Rev. Lyman Beecher perhaps the best expression of Protestant Whiggery. I wonder about this designation, however. Beecher functioned almost exclusively in the sphere of the church—as pastor, theologian, evangelist, and seminary president. He did assume leadership among many of the benevolent empire's voluntary associations, but always as a church figure, as a spokesman of the "spiritual" rather than the "secular" realm. His overall leadership was therefore limited by definition. Theodore Frelinghuysen, on the other hand, suffered from no such limitation. "Secular" leadership based on Christian principles was his forte. As such, he is, in my opinion, a more comprehensive representative of a culturally transforming Protestant Whiggery in antebellum America.

Leadership

Evangelical Protestant America did need leadership in the late 1830's. What we call secular humanism today (irreligion) was on the rise, and the alarm had to be sounded. *An Inquiry into the Moral and Religious Character of the American Government* was a significant warning. Even if somewhat overstated at points, it raised many of the correct issues and highlighted the proper path to follow: nations as well as individuals must travel the road of godliness. Each must "return to the primary spirit of government [the spirit of Christianity] ere the doom of the nations that forget God becomes our own."

One other enigma, however, must also be confronted regarding the book: Frelinghuysen's choice to have it published anonymously. Why would he be so "modest," especially when this secret was no secret at all? His contemporaries assumed Frelinghuysen's authorship from the beginning.

One possibility is that the contents were so controversial that he was simply afraid to claim authorship. But this makes little sense. Frelinghuysen was certainly no coward; much of his career had already been a courageous stance on unpopular and controversial subjects. The contents, moreover, were largely a restatement of previous pronouncements: an 1831 speech before a debate society came to many of the same conclusions.

Some critics might suggest nativism as a possible reason for anonymity. The mayor's concern for Catholic immigrants might have made him hesitate to place his name on such a clearly "Protestant" book, for fear of retaliation by immigrants at the ballot box. This is an illogical answer. Even if he had been a nativist—which he was not—the opposite is a more likely tactic, namely, acknowledgement of authorship in order to benefit from the tide of nativism then beginning to rise throughout the Northeast. Riding this wave could have secured him in the mayoralty and perhaps even propelled him back into the national political spotlight. Choosing such a politically "low road" was never an option for Theodore Frelinghuysen.

The final and most compelling possibility relates to Frelinghuysen's personal dilemma over a potential change of vocation. By the late 1830's, Frelinghuysen had already spent three decades as a private attorney, attorney general, U.S. senator, and mayor. He was beginning to tire of both the bar and politics. There are also some indications of health problems brought on by physical exhaustion. He began to contemplate a change of scenery to find relief from the hectic pace of public life. In this context, higher education no doubt appeared attractive as a vocational alternative.

In 1838 he first considered seriously the field of educational leadership, an option which he chose the following year when he assumed the chancellorship of New York University. Thus the time of the difficult personal decision coincided closely with the writing, publication, and initial exposure of the book. It is likely that this coincidence strongly suggested anonymity to the mayor. While controversy was acceptable for politics, he probably reasoned, it was less appropriate for education. While political leadership presupposed sharp divisions and heated debate, educational leadership required unity and rational dialogue—especially, as he learned during these months, when a university like N.Y.U. was seeking financial stability. If my supposition is correct, being "above politics" might have suddenly seemed advantageous to him.

I am not entirely satisfied though with my own analysis. Remaining anonymous cannot be entirely justified in terms of leadership. In retrospect, perhaps he should have placed his name on the title page and accepted whatever effects followed from its being published. After all, wouldn't that also have been characteristic of good leadership?

* * * * * * *

Discussion Questions

1. Frelinghuysen attacked the Jeffersonian-Jacksonian tradition in American politics. Do you agree that this tradition was the cause of most of the problems in antebellum America? Which party today exemplifies this tradition? If Frelinghuysen were alive today, what would be his party preference and why?

2. To what extent is anti-Catholicism and hatred of immigrants a force in American politics today? What should be our response as Christians to such examples of political "nativism"?

3. I suggested that denominational problems undermined the cause of Protestant reform during Frelinghuysen's lifetime. To what extent is this true today? Should Christian leaders strive specifically for political unity in spite of denominational disparity? Why or why not?

4. How does a "theocracy" function? Should America be a theocracy? Why or why not?

5. Was America, as Frelinghuysen believed, largely a Christian nation during the colonial and Revolutionary eras? Should we strive to be a Christian nation today? Why or why not?

6. Is our political system "Christian"? If so, what are its most positive features? If not, how would you describe our system?

7. Is our Constitution atheistic because it doesn't mention God? Should it mention God or Christ? What do you think of Frelinghuysen's notion that the Constitution "presumes" the existence of God?

8. Should individuals and nations (states) obey God because of expediency, because of the blessings which they assume should follow obedience?

9. Are Christians more moral than others, thus deserving of political leadership?

10. Do you think there is ever a case for anonymity for Christian leaders? Under what circumstances would it occur? Was Frelinghuysen justified in publishing his book anonymously?

Chapter 7

Colonization:
A Case of Missing The Boat?

Avarice has, in twenty-five years, robbed from this suffering country [Africa], two million of her children—and shall
Christian America, the favored of heaven—the land of
liberty, and enterprise, and charity, be told that philanthro-
py, cannot achieve more than this wicked spirit....We can
send to Africa all her sons—and we must—or endure a
reproach that will be the shame and the curse of our country.

[But] exigencies of circumstance may properly prevent [slav-
ery's] prompt abolition....

[Colonization is a] first step toward a radical reform.
                              —Theodore Frelinghuysen, 1824

The excitement mounted as the conferees gathered during the Christ-
mas holidays of 1816. Rarely had the nation's capital seen such a prestigious and determined assemblage: Chief Justice John Marshall came
to protect the Constitution; President-elect James Monroe attended to
strengthen the fledgling Republic; John Randolph came to guard the
interests of the South as did Daniel Webster for the North; and Henry
Clay presided, in part, to uphold the interests of his native West. What
topic would cause such concern, and who had convened this meeting
of heavyweights, only five of whom I have just named?

The topic was slavery and what to do about it. The slave trade had
ended by law in 1807, but slavery itself remained firmly entrenched
in the South and in the border states. Since the Constitution was unlikely to be amended to abolish slavery, what alternatives existed? Were
there any options, they pondered, to perpetuating the status quo? The
convener was Rev. Robert Finley of New Jersey, and he had a solution: gradual emancipation of negroes followed by the colonization of
freemen back in their ancestral African homeland!

Finley was a likely candidate for leadership of a colonization movement. He had been trained by noted antislavery spokesman John Wither-

spoon, had recently returned from a visit to South Carolina where he observed firsthand the evils of slavery, and had even more recently finished a text for a pamphlet entitled "Thoughts on the Colonization of Free Blacks." In a February 15, 1815, letter to a friend, he predicted confidently that colonization would benefit all concerned. The nation's remaining slaves would be better treated, and Africa would benefit from a "civilized and Christianized" people.

Finley's confidence was no doubt based partly on the success of a British project similar to it launched at Sierra Leone in the 1790's by William Wilberforce and other evangelicals. In fact, when the American Colonization Society was formed by many within this same group on December 28, 1816, the hope was first expressed that America's freemen would be allowed to emigrate to the British colony. Only later, when Britain balked, did attention shift to the formation of an American-sponsored colony located in adjacent "Liberia."

The precise location of the colony was not the matter of prime concern, however. The overriding issue was public relations, how to convince Americans of the wisdom and practicality of the proposal. Having VIP's in the organization helped the image, but few of them did the actual selling. What Finley needed was an engaging and persuasive young man to carry on the fight in the corridors of power while he departed the Northeast to preside over the newly-formed University of Georgia. (He left within a few months.) His former star pupil Theodore Frelinghuysen being such a man, he chose him as a close confidant as he fathered the American Colonization Society!

In subsequent years few leaders showed as much devotion to the cause of colonization as did the New Jersey statesman. In the weeks following the winter conclave, for example, Frelinghuysen, as the newly-appointed attorney general for the state, supported Finley's efforts to launch a New Jersey chapter of the national organization. He remained loyal to the state chapter throughout his lifetime and later served for many years as vice-president of the American Colonization Society. Ralph Gurley, long-time secretary of the national organization, recalled in 1862 how Frelinghuysen had on many occasions given legal counsel to the society and how generous he had been with his financial contributions (usually giving $100 per year). "Probably no man in the country," concluded Gurley, "[had] exerted a more cheerful or more widespread influence for the public good....Africa will remember him forever as one of her truest and best friends."

From our twentieth-century perspective we have to ask why Frelinghuysen was so devoted to the cause of colonization. And what does such commitment mean for our analysis of Theodore Frelinghuysen as a Christian leader?

At the outset, I must admit that proving normative leadership on this issue is difficult. All morality and "history" seem to argue against

Frelinghuysen. The modern American mentality is so hostile to slavery that abolitionism seems in retrospect the only ethical position. Still, a "reasonable" case can be made for colonization and thus for a demonstration of a degree of leadership on Frelinghuysen's part.

What is needed first is a more accurate recollection of history which, I suggest, will shed a more positive light on Frelinghuysen's position. Between 1815 and 1830 many American leaders—excluding some Quakers—looked favorably upon colonization. Both northern and southern philanthropists found the idea appealing, so Frelinghuysen was not alone in his defense of colonization. Even evangelical leaders like Arthur and Lewis Tappan initially joined with the philanthropists, as did the youthful abolitionist zealot, William Lloyd Garrison. Colonization, in short, seemed to many a workable and benevolent idea. Only after the early 1830's when colonization began to lose major support did some of its internal inconsistencies, strange alliances, and Liberian liabilities surface as major detriments to the movement. Even so, the idea of colonization offered hope—as we shall see—to other prominent Americans than just Theodore Frelinghuysen.

Numerous reasons can be found for Frelinghuysen's particular support of the idea of colonization. The following summary is taken from several sources, especially his 1824 article on colonization and his 1838 book.

1. No listing of reasons would be complete without reference to his mentor, Robert Finley. Even loyalty to Henry Clay and admiration for the memory of Wilberforce paled when compared to Frelinghuysen's love for the New Jersey teacher and clergyman. "[I am] much indebted to his early counsels," he acknowledged, "[a] grateful pupil." This was especially the case when he contemplated the colonization scheme, a plan which was "novel," "bold," and "magnanimous." Only a man as visionary as Finley, Frelinghuysen confessed, could have proposed such a far-reaching solution to the tragedy of slavery in America.

2. Scholars disagree on Frelinghuysen's approach to the morality of slavery. A few, like William Hunt, suggest that slavery "[did] not seem to have distressed Frelinghuysen or even interested him as a moral issue." Others, like William Demarest, come to the opposite conclusion: "His full hatred of slavery was well established." Demarest's assessment is the correct one and easy to prove. Here are just a few of Frelinghuysen's statements about slavery:

> Here [in America] where freedom flourishes has grown up a polluted idol, relieved by no virtues, and more odious and remorseless than the Juggernaut of the Heathen. On the same breeze have been borne to the ear, the grateful shouts of American Freemen and the heart-sickening groans of subjected slaves.... Conscience [concludes] that slavery can not be justified.   1824

....slavery is an evil not to be tolerated in Christian principles. I most heartily grant....it should be removed.

1833

Slavery is against us. [It is here by the] inconsiderate wick-
edness of other times. [We hope for progress] so that the
point of ultimate desire and destination [freedom] be the more
safely and surely....attained.

1838

[Slavery is the result of] a state of moral evil in the minds
and characters of men, that calls yet more vehemently for
redress.

1838

The Moloch of the seas [the slave trade] is destroyed; the
Moloch of the land is now doomed. His day has come.

1838

As a great moral and social evil [slavery] is....a gravely
momentous subject.

1855

In sum, Frelinghuysen clearly considered slavery to be immoral and
unChristian. Emancipation and colonization were therefore for him a
moral imperative.

3. Frelinghuysen had, it appears, a guilty conscience about slavery.
Evidence suggests that slavery was his by "inheritance,"
i.e., a part of his family tradition. Perhaps some of his neighbors were
also participating in this moral evil. And his beloved New Jersey had
not completely abolished slavery. The "gradual emancipation" begun
in 1804 worked so slowly that it was still possible (though rare) to own
slaves even at the onset of the Civil War. He no doubt felt a sharp twinge
of personal embarrassment by all these developments and looked upon
colonization as one way to make amends.

4. Frelinghuysen's confidence swelled because the benevolent empire made room for the goal of colonization. In fact, during the early
years the American Colonization Society was considered to be an in-
tegral part of the massive campaign for moral reformation. What better
way to assuage a righteous God, it was argued, than to wipe the stain
of slavery from the social fabric and leave no living reminders behind?

He gained even greater comfort from the support forthcoming from
particular religious denominations. Very shortly after the inception of
the society, the Presbyterian Church gave its blessing to the colonization principle. The Presbyterians were imitated in 1825 by action of
the Synod of the Dutch Reformed Church. As an evangelical and a Calvinist who identified with these two institutions, nothing could have been
more pleasing to him.

5. Evangelism cannot be overlooked as a cause for support of colonization. Frelinghuysen realized that despite the horrors of human bondage many slaves had experienced sincere conversion to Christianity.

Why not then introduce Christianity and Christian civilization into Africa through regenerated freemen? "Every cargo of emancipated black men that you send home [to Liberia]," he prophesied before the New Jersey Colonization Society in 1824, "will be the pioneers of the benighted countrymen—may be the instructors of their youth, and the preachers of righteousness." Liberia could become a "free Christian commonwealth" which would lead to the eventual evangelization of the entire pagan continent. Does such a plan sound strange to our evangelical ears today? If so, we must keep in mind that in antebellum America the very thought of sending missionaries to the "dark" continent was a novel idea indeed; Africa was just then beginning to be opened up to the gospel. Frelinghuysen's proposal gains more credibility when seen in this light.

6. Colonization seemed the only feasible solution because of constitutional limitations. Due to the Constitution and its prescription of federalism, "Slavery...is a domestic concern that Congress has not the right or power to interfere with in its legislation," Frelinghuysen declared in 1844. "Politically," he acknowledged as late as 1855, "we agreed [in the Constitution] to leave it where we found it, and that was with the slaveholding states."

Constitutionally, America was in a bind. The document Frelinghuysen loved so dearly and the political system that so satisfied his thirst for order and harmony only complicated the moral dilemma surrounding slavery:

> What the *political* action is which the Constitution PRESCRIBES for the removal of slavery, we are yet to learn; nor is it easy to imagine a federal principle adequate to that result, and, at the same time, compatible with the "sovereignty of each state to legislate *exclusively*" on the subject, and the disclaimer of any right of Congress, under the *present* national compact, to interfere with any of the Slave States on this momentous subject.

Colonization, because it dealt only with slaves who had already been freed, was an answer but a partial one in an imperfect world.

7. The Union too was imperfect but had to be preserved. According to Joseph Folsom, Frelinghuysen's "strongest endeavor, in the face of the new crisis [slavery], was to prevent the disruption of the Union." As a former-Whig-turned-Republican, he spoke out strongly in the mid-1850's in defense of the need for the perpetuation of the union's experiment in constitutional liberty. "May no rash hand mar its glory," he pleaded, "or dare disturb its foundation....Should not the smiles of God's favor towards us [in the past] hush the murmurs of discontent, and persuade us rather to...hope?" By "rash hand" he wasn't referring to Nat Turner and other slave rebels, but to William Lloyd Garrison, the Tappans, and the specter of radical abolitionism.

Colonization, Abolitionism, and the South

Why such fear of abolitionism? How could Frelinghuysen cheerfully announce during the 1844 campaign that he was not an abolitionist? Were the goals of the abolitionists and those who favored colonization so dissimilar? To answer these and similar questions is to probe even more deeply into the underlying reasons for Frelinghuysen's support of colonization.

The key to Frelinghuysen's animosity toward abolitionists is linked to the transformation which occurred in the antislavery position of William Lloyd Garrison, the Tappan brothers, and other evangelicals. Initially enamored of colonization, they turned against it vehemently in the late 1820's and early 1830's. Garrison, for example, the same man who canonized Frelinghuysen in an 1830 poem, also included a footnote to the poem which read: "It is painful to be compelled to say, that the cause pursued by Mr. Frelinghuysen [re: Indian rights] in relation to the rights and the wrongs of our colored population, has not been such as to justify the unqualified eulogium conveyed in these lines." A few weeks previous to the footnote Garrison had found colonization to be incompatible with the aims of the antislavery proponents.

> What has the Society accomplished?...has it, in any degree, sustained its high pretensions? or made good one of its numberless and extravagant proclamations? or taken away a fraction from the "sum total"? or made any visible impression upon the growth of slavery? Assuredly not. . . . And yet is the the colonization mania—such the implicit confidence reposed in the operations of the Society—that no demonstration of its inefficiency...can shake the faith of its advocates.

As the 1830's unfolded, the Tappans led many evangelicals in abandoning the colonization strategy. Even after American abolitionism split in the late 1830's—pitting the Tappans against Garrison—colonization never returned as a serious option to its former adherents. In fact, many former supporters no doubt applauded the sentiments expressed by William Jay in his "open letter" to Frelinghuysen in October, 1844:

> You have lent the influence of your name, associated as it is with the religious zeal and benevolence of the nation, to the cause of slavery....Before long, we shall each of us be called to give account of our stewardship...involving...upholding or resisting that stupendous accumulation of sin and misery, American slavery. Most earnestly do I wish, sir, that...you [could soon] exclaim, "I am an abolitionist, and I thank God I am."

What sincere supporter of colonization would not be unnerved by such an arrow driven into the heart by a fellow Christian?

Much more was at stake, however, than wounded egos. Frelinghuysen honestly believed that abolitionism was the wrong path to travel. In his opinion, it led to suffering for all concerned, the Union, the two regions, and the two races involved.

Four errors in particular plagued the abolitionist ideology, according to Frelinghuysen. First, abolitionism as it matured in the 1830's and 1840's called ever more stridently for *immediate* emancipation. All attempts at incrementalism, whether through colonization schemes or anything else, were denounced as sinful. It must be "now" and it must be "total," screamed Garrison. Second, many abolitionists implied that the southern way of life was fundamentally corrupt and worthless because it had from the outset based everything on the oppressive system of human bondage. Third, belief number two produced the corollary not as strongly adhered to by Garrison himself that the northern way of life was sound, one into which negroes could easily be integrated following emancipation. Fourth, many abolitionists seemed to accept the basic goodness of human nature, or at least its perfectibility, as long as environmental shortcomings were eliminated.

Frelinghuysen rejected immediate emancipation because it was extremely dangerous. Here is his prediction of what it would unleash:

> But cast your eye over the cities and plantations of the South...[Can we ask] our brethren to deluge their land with the horrid scenes that would certainly follow the liberation of a[n]...ignorant and irritated population restrained by no principles, and with every bad passion of the heart inflamed[?] It would, in effect, be to ask of them, after unsheathing the sword, to place it in the grasp of rapine and murder, and invoke their vengeance....
>
> Suddenly to emancipate the millions of the South, or to raise them to the proud dignity of freemen, in the bosom of their white Society, is not their duty. It would be the madness of self-destruction.

Racism did not make him paint such a lurid picture; he did not believe that negroes were inherently morally inferior to whites. But they had been terribly mistreated for many generations, and this abuse had taken its toll. What other condition could the nation expect from any race which had experienced similar oppression? His conclusion, nonetheless, was still positive: "Give the African fair play [opportunity] and then judge whether his head or his heart be below our standard."

For Frelinghuysen, gradualism, not immediate emancipation, was the best path to follow. God's method had always been the kind, patient persuasiveness of the gospel: "That gentle spirit has...effected changes, which a more military demeanor would not only have failed to accomplish, but would doubtless have interfered with and delayed, if not prevented." The South would only respond to persuasion, not violence:

> Men are not to be personally won even to [God's] allegi-
> ance against their will: much less should we expect them to
> relinquish their possessions, or change their long-established
> institutions, till their own eyes have been opened to the
> propriety of doing so.

Why so much confidence in gradualism? Because it worked. He often noted how a moderate approach had helped create an environment in which the slave trade was ended by 1807, where many northern states had abolished slavery by the 1830's and where southern sympathy for emancipation had grown during the first three decades of the nineteenth century. More progress was forthcoming, he predicted, if only patience were practiced.

Frelinghuysen did not believe that the South was evil incarnate or that all virtue resided in the North. Apart from the curse of slavery, the southern way of life had many positive features: commitments to order, the Judeo-Christian tradition, classical culture, and the nuclear family, for example. The North, on the other hand, was becoming increasingly "pluralistic" (less uniquely Protestant), materialistic, even secular in public affairs. Unfortunately, many Christians were unaware of these developments, still clinging to an older model justifying their simplistic analyses of the differences in the two cultures. A failure on the part of northern Christians to recognize the increasing seculariza-tion of the North led to the following irony.

> Some have been guilty of great injustice in the feelings they
> have cherished toward the South; and have declaimed against
> slavery as if, really, all Christian feelings, principle, and duty
> ranged on the north of the Delaware! *There was never a*
> *greater or more humiliating mistake.*

Ignorance and pride were thus, in Frelinghuysen's judgment, the chief culprits.

Finally, pride, sinful pride, had closed the eyes of Northerners to the "awful truth" about universal human nature. We were all fallen crea-tures, preached the Calvinist. No one of us could claim any righteous-ness of his own; no one could justly locate sin in some far away place—like the South. Sin was thoroughly at home also in the northern heart. This insightful recognition on Frelinghuysen's part contributed to his strongest argument for colonization. If sin rested comfortably in the northern breast, what an illusion to think that negro freemen would be welcomed with open arms beyond the Delaware. Wouldn't sin con-tinue to hold sway? "As American citizens," he fearfully projected, "these men never can be free. And as American freemen, they never would be valuable." Was there any basis for his fear? Yes, in the actu-al history of negro freemen in the North! Despite the efforts of benevo-

66

lent societies and compassionate individuals to care for them and to facilitate their integration into northern society, little progress had been made. Racism precluded such toleration. Tragically, negro freemen remained "a separate, degraded, scorned, and humbled people. With a line of demarcation drawn deep and broad; and durable as time." Wouldn't it be better, he implored, for slaves and freemen to return to "the land of their fathers"? Wouldn't the gift of "fair play" be maximized in Africa?

I have tried to be as sympathetic as possible to Frelinghuysen's rationale or rationalization for colonization. I think his case was a reasonable one in the sense that it could have been adopted by a reasonable Christian living in antebellum America, experiencing the limits of the historical knowledge of his time. I have suggested his insight peaked with the recognition that racism in the North might make a mockery out of the facile assertion that freemen would be warmly embraced once slavery ended. Post-Civil War history has painfully shown how closely on target was his prediction. Moreover, his confession of slavery as a moral issue and his desire to see Africa evangelized were also progressive features of his colonization plan.

But several weaknesses also characterized his proposal. An inordinate love of the Constitution, of federalism, even of the Union itself blurred his vision. And "gradualism" perhaps played too great a role in his thinking. What a vague term. Just how gradual is gradual? It was all too easy for him and others in the Colonization Society to call for "patience" on the part of slaves. Sometimes the gospel demands a sword of justice rather than a "gentle spirit."

Finally, Frelinghuysen was guilty of exaggerating the positive features of life in Liberia. In his public statements he sang the praises of both the Colonization Society and the colonial administration, overlooking most discordant notes. Yet, even during his lifetime Liberia floundered. P. J. Staudenraus has shown in his study, *The African Colonization Movement* (1961), how Liberia lurched forward from crisis to crisis, never financially stable and rarely welcoming more than a few hundred immigrants per year. As vice-president of the American Colonization Society during many of these crucial years, Frelinghuysen surely knew of its trials and tribulations. But he chose to accentuate the positive. Maybe he had learned too well the responsibilities of "public relations."

Conclusion

What has often been overlooked in this issue are the dissimilarities between abolitionists and colonizationists. On the surface, their goal appeared identical: total emancipation. Beneath the surface, however, sharp differences in their programs emerged, both in means and in ends. Abolitionists generally sought immediate manumission and integration

67

of negroes into a free, individualistic, capitalistic society. Colonizationists, on the other hand, urged patience and held out as their final solution segregation of the races by way of emigration to Africa or some other suitable place.

Therein lies the rub. We as a people, Christians too, are so committed today to cultural integration and individual freedom rights that Frelinghuysen's alternative, no doubt, seems immoral. The judgment is largely correct, and it does point out the difficulty of rehabilitating his name and reputation. In fact, I'm inclined to say that his support of colonization is the principal reason why he is so little remembered today. Few evangelical and Reformed historians and social scientists recall the name of the man who generally was so famous and loved in antebellum America. As the decades unfolded, research and scholarship concentrated on abolitionism, not colonization. Subsequently, popular opinion followed in its wake.

This neglect is unfortunate, not because colonization should be wholeheartedly defended today but because we have consequently lost touch with our historical roots. We have lost touch with a man whose life to some extent can serve as a contemporary model of leadership. Not a perfect model but a guiding light nonetheless.

How mysterious and ironic history sometimes is. What if Frelinghuysen had been elected vice-president in 1844 and then gone on to the presidency? Or what if he had been born just a few years later, in the early nineteenth century? This last question is not entirely trivial speculation, for there was another man whose lifetime overlapped Frelinghuysen's and whose characteristics were strikingly similar to his own. This man too was a lawyer, a politician, a Whig-turned-Republican. He too had a strong religious commitment and personally found slavery immoral. He too sought to preserve the Union and hesitated to follow the abolitionist line of denunciation of the South. He too found the idea of colonization appealing, so much so that even as late as the time of Frelinghuysen's death (early in 1862), colonization schemes had not been completely abandoned.

His name was Abraham Lincoln.

* * * * * * *

Discussion Questions

1. Did Frelinghuysen rely too much on his personal connection with Robert Finley in determining his stand on slavery? What are the dangers of letting admiration for others shape our own moral positions?

2. The Presbyterian and Dutch Reformed denominations came out in support of colonization. Should they denominationally have taken such a stance? Or should they have avoided taking a position on slav-

ery in favor of individual action? When is it proper for churches to take moral or political stands? Give examples from our contemporary world.

3. Was evangelism of Africa a proper reason for supporting colonization? To what extent did this show leadership on the part of Frelinghuysen?

4. Was the Constitution fatally flawed because of its approach to slavery? How should this flaw affect our attitude toward the Constitution today? Name a major moral or political problem with the Constitution today. How should that problem be solved?

5. With respect to the question of slavery, did Frelinghuysen love the Union too dearly?

6. Frelinghuysen was stung by the 1844 attack by William Jay. How should Christians respond to criticism by other believers? Give an example from recent history of a proper response by a Christian politician or leader.

7. Was Frelinghuysen's reluctance to condemn the South harshly justified?

8. What do you think of Frelinghuysen's principle of gradualism as a solution to distressing moral concerns? Name an issue today about which gradualism rather than immediate transformation is the appropriate answer.

9. The lynchpin of Frelinghuysen's argument for colonization was the racism of Northerners—of which many were "unaware." Evaluate his judgment of the North in light of post-Civil War history. To what extent is northern "racism" still a problem today? Give examples.

10. Could Frelinghuysen have become a Lincoln?

11. In the final analysis, did Frelinghuysen "miss the boat" on slavery by supporting colonization? Why or why not?

Chapter 8

Benevolent Emperor

The charity of the gospel is its most beautiful, most distinguishing characteristic.
—Theodore Frelinghuysen, 1838

Let us ponder...the interesting truth, that our boasted liberties will not long survive the wreck of our public morals.
—Theodore Frelinghuysen, 1831

But the antebellum period was the great time of evangelical triumph. These were the days above all when the "Evangelical United Front" took up the manifold causes of moral reform, missionary advance, and humanitarian reform....Its aim was to bring the gospel to all America and to heathen lands abroad, but primarily it hoped to make America the world's great example of a truly Protestant republic. The institution by which this vast program was carried out was the interdenominational voluntary association.
—Sidney Ahlstrom, 1972

It was the spring of 1837, and already the deleterious effects of the economic recession were evident to concerned Christians. Money was becoming scarce, the money so urgently needed to fund the evangelical agencies which together formed the "benevolent empire." Without funds, how could the righteous cause continue?

At the same time, the American Board of Commissioners for Foreign Missions was holding its annual meeting in Newark, New Jersey. Their financial plight too was serious. Gifts had declined to the point where the officers of the society projected "a very serious and unmanageable debt." Speaker after speaker took note of the alarming situation until the audience was unusually agitated. It seemed to some that the meeting was falling apart.

Then Theodore Frelinghuysen rose to take charge. The newly-elected mayor had been sitting in the audience listening to the ever-increasing tone of dread until he could stomach no more. The American Board had been his "first love" as a young man, the first to receive his attention and financial support, and he felt compelled to speak out.

He spoke spontaneously for one-half hour. He appealed for calm and for faith: God's Kingdom would survive this crisis as it had survived all others. He also called for sacrifice, for he acknowledged that the American Board did need additional funds during those difficult months. And why should Christians dig even deeper into their pockets? "For the Savior's honor and the salvation of a perishing world," came his answer. Frelinghuysen spoke with such force and enthusiasm that the packed house, according to one observer, was "spellbound," "overwhelmed" with emotion, ready once again to dedicate themselves to reach out to the world for the King!

The benevolent empire—of which the American Board was an early example—was not treated very kindly by historians and other researchers during the 1950's and 1960's. John R. Bodo (1954), Charles C. Cole, Jr. (1954), Charles I. Foster (1960), and Clifford S. Griffin (1960), among others, all wrote essentially negative appraisals of the massive antebellum effort by conservative evangelicals to "Christianize America" through missionary outreach and moral reform. Perhaps "McCarthyism" in America had something to do with their motivation; they were perhaps overreacting to the conservative paranoia of the times, seeing in the antebellum program a precursor of the "witchhunts" they endured in the middle and late 1950's. At any rate, the picture they painted is not very flattering. Benevolent societies, in essence, were masks behind which individuals hid, individuals who were not really interested in social improvement but in social control—in preserving their declining status and regaining the control they believed was once theirs in American society. More specifically, the critics proclaimed the following weaknesses of the empire: (1) it had a narrow geographical base of support (largely New England); (2) the clergy played an inordinate guiding role; (3) lurking just beneath the surface was the desire to link the "church" closely with the state, just short of establishment; (4) "good works" were not really important to many of the movements and denominations in the empire; and (5) their "reforms" were largely superficial in terms of their impact on society.

More recent scholarship, however, has challenged all of these contentions. Lois W. Banner, Donald G. Matthews, Daniel Walker Howe, and others, for example, make a convincing case that the benevolent empire had a broad base of popular support and a wide range of leadership, was hostile to all forms of entanglement of church and state, was universally popular, and enacted culturally significant reforms. Rather than being a selfish call for a return to theocracy (Bodo), the empire was, concludes Banner, a sincere effort "to insure the success of the American republic and ultimately to attain a stable democratic order."

Critics and revisionists agree, however, on four important points. First, the benevolent empire benefited from the religious sentiment unleashed by the Second Great Awakening, which began in the 1790's and recurred sporadically but powerfully until the mid-1830's. "The Revival," notes Donald Matthews, "...promised a 'positive outcome in an uncertain situation' [post-Revolutionary instability] for it proposed to make men better by putting them into direct contact with God. It also provided values or goals for which to work and codes which regulated behavior giving ideological as well as social order to life." Second, the empire—even if somewhat superficial in the eyes of its critics—was composed of an impressive array of societies, dealing with many different kinds of issues. The Bible and missions, temperance, colonization/abolition, paupers, education, peace, and women's rights all received attention by becoming the focal points of various specific reform movements and organizations. Third, reform was undertaken largely by voluntary associations, not by the institutional church. And these associations frequently worked together in a network of "interlocking directorates," i.e., they shared many of the same leaders. Fourth, Calvinists, especially Presbyterians but also the Dutch Reformed, were the most prominent leaders of the various societies.

When we look for an individual who embodied the above four points, our attention is immediately drawn to Theodore Frelinghuysen. He was a proponent of the Second Great Awakening, well befitting the descendant of New Jersey's premier revivalist of the First Awakening, Theodore J. Frelinghuysen. His interest in missions and moral reform was encyclopedic, and he championed voluntary associations. In the words of Joseph Folsom, "Mr. Frelinghuysen was an earnest advocate of the claims of organized Christian benevolence, and fully merited the statement that no American layman was ever associated with so many great national organizations of religion and charity as he." Finally, he was an evangelical Calvinist, a Reformed Christian who worshiped and functioned throughout his life in a "Presbyterian" context.

What follows is an examination of his major contributions to the cause of Christian benevolence.

The American Board of Commissioners for Foreign Missions

The American Board began in 1810 with an ambitious goal: to reach the whole pagan world with the message of the gospel. Its first efforts were in India, Ceylon, the American West, and the Sandwich Islands. These initial steps, though, were small since money and leadership were in short supply. Barely $1,000 was raised the first year, for example, by a board composed of only nine men.

Yet the Board prospered as the public caught the missionary vision. By 1850 the financial panic was a dim memory and yearly receipts totaled $250,000, with the leadership expanding to 178 "corporate members," directing between 6,000 and 7,000 honorary members. The annual meeting that same year drew 300 men and women from sixteen states. The American Board by mid-century, according to one sympathetic historian, "had taken its place among the honored and commanding institutions of the land." Fittingly, its president was Theodore Frelinghuysen.

Frelinghuysen's relationship with the American Board spanned nearly one-half century. Learning of it soon after its founding, he began a lifelong habit of financial and prayer support. His dedication was rewarded in 1826 by his nomination as a corporate member, a position he maintained for several years. Between 1826 and 1841, he was frequent in attendance at the board's annual meetings. In 1841 he was chosen president, serving with distinction until 1857. His choice and tenure, according to contemporaries, was popular with the whole constituency.

Frelinghuysen's commitment to the American Board derived from his concern for the souls of those who did not know Christ. Because reaching them was his highest priority, missionaries received his greatest adulation.

> When you beheld them [he told a supportive audience in 1818] consenting to form permanent relations with strangers and savages, in a pagan land...and this to proclaim a Savior's righteousness to ears that never knew his name, did you not feel with an overwhelming emotion, that there was [glory] in this work?

In short, working closely with this missionary board was a great privilege because it allowed him to glimpse "the first streaks of the morning, the sure tokens [converted souls] of that coming glory which the Sun of Righteousness shall shed upon this benighted and sin-stricken world."

Frelinghuysen resigned the presidency of the American Board in 1857, not because of a change of heart, but because his denomination, the Dutch Reformed Church, had decided to form its own missionary agency. This development grieved him somewhat. He had long been committed to non- or interdenominational voluntary societies as the best vehicle for reaching and changing the world. "When our several Christian denominations...all labored together on benighted and heathen fields," he said in 1857, "it struck me as a beautiful type of our blessed Master's religion in its aspects toward these lands of darkness."

Disappointment, though, did not damage his loyalty toward missions. Almost immediately after resignation he was appointed by his denomination to its Board of Foreign Missions. By the time of his death in 1862, he had also become president of this board!

The American Bible Society

Theodore Frelinghuysen realized that missionaries were empowered not only by the Spirit but by the Word of God. An intimate relationship with the American Bible Society was thus a natural one. "The American Bible Society," he proclaimed in 1857, "reaches the great mind of our country, and brings it into communion with principles and promises which God has connected with all that is pure and... hopeful...for eternity. If the Bible did no other service, its clear revelations of man's immortal destiny would be beyond all price."

The Bible Society was formed in 1816 with the ultimate goal of worldwide distribution of God's Word in several languages. Wanting to participate in this noble cause, the New Jerseyite kept abreast of developments within the Bible Society and made frequent financial contributions. His interest was appreciated within the governing circles: he was first chosen as vice-president in 1830, a position he held until 1846 when the voting members unanimously selected him as president, a position he kept for the rest of his life. His purpose in accepting the presidency was clearly stated in 1846: to increase the circulation of "that sacred Book, which reveals the best and only lasting hope for ourselves, our country, and the world." President Frelinghuysen's commitment to the Bible Society was remarkable. He gave opening addresses at every anniversary during his tenure. "They were delivered," noted one contemporary, "with that silver-tongued eloquence of which he was a master, and on certain occasions produced grand effects upon his audiences...." While he served as chancellor of New York University during the 1840's, each May, for the Bible Society anniversary, students received three days' vacation from ordinary activities to enable them to participate in the Society's work. Even on the eve of the Civil War (May 9, 1861), he could take solace only in the work of agencies like the Bible Society:

> While there is much to alarm and afflict us in the political agitations of our country, one thing is of special comfort. In the cause of the Bible Society, we are still one—bound together by the bonds of Christian kindness, animated by like hopes, earnest in like purposes, and cheered by the same sympathies.

There were four reasons for such unwavering loyalty to the American Bible Society that rested on the foundations of Frelinghuysen's own faith: (1) the Bible brought human beings face to face with their Savior; (2) the Bible was the only foundation for the faith and life of young people; (3) the Bible, when properly interpreted and obeyed, produced national prosperity and peace; and (4) the Bible promoted Christian benevolence. What force but the Bible, he concluded, "disrobes self-

ishness of her odious garb...moderates the pursuit of ambition, recti-
fies the struggle for ascendency, and...purifies the motives of human
action[?]'' While he worked hard and diligently for all his benevolent
societies, there was perhaps only a little exaggeration in a friend's 1862
judgment that Frelinghuysen ''regarded as the highest honor conferred
on him by men—the presidency of the American Bible Society.''

The American Tract Society

God's Kingdom could also be advanced by the distribution of religious literature and literature urging specific moral reform. For this
reason, Frelinghuysen was a strong supporter of tract societies, especially the American Tract Society, founded in 1823 from the older New
England Tract Society. Once again, he gave numerous addresses on be-
half of the tract societies, both as an interested layman and as president
of the American Tract Society—a position he held from 1842 to 1848.

One address in particular points out Frelinghuysen's attitude toward
tract societies. It was delivered at the Broadway Tabernacle at the anniversary of the City Tract Society in December, 1836. The ''tract missionary,'' he noted, should expect persecution for his efforts. ''To go
alone into the by-paths of sin; to approach the thoughtless in the world
of fashion [is to] meet the scorn and taunts of ridicule....'' It was,
nonetheless, the missionary's joyful duty to reach out to others even
if the world did not understand. And the outstretched hand offered not
only salvation but also hope for transformed lives. As proof, Frelinghuysen recounted the story of a hardened criminal who was transformed
by the kindness of a tract missionary. The prisoner confessed that when
the hand of friendship was offered, ''it is the first time in forty years
that I have heard the language of kindness, and it overwhelms me.''
This life was changed by commitment and the power of love, Frelinghuysen happily recalled. In addition, Frelinghuysen expressed and drew
great comfort from the promise that God sees, cares, and rewards: we
will all ''begin to learn of the heights and depths of the recompense
that grace awards to those who have done good to souls.''

Frelinghuysen was still giving leadership to the American Tract Society
well into the 1850's. One example is worth noting. In 1856 the society
was being torn apart by the slavery issue. The antagonists were a
proslavery Boston supporter, Rev. Nehemiah Adams, on the one hand,
and the rabid abolitionist tract members on the other. At the point when
emotions seemed ready to explode, Frelinghuysen was asked by Tract
Society officers to help form a committee to resolve the dispute. After
much discussion, a compromise was reached wherein the society agreed
to reject the abolitionist answer while remaining free to publish tracts
condemning whatever moral evils and vices slavery obviously produced.
The Frelinghuysen style of leadership is clearly evident from his recon-

ciliation of such warring factions.

Frelinghuysen wanted the benevolent societies internally to be examples of God's reconciling love. His efforts were at least partially successful, as can be seen from the 1862 tribute by the Tract Society's secretary, William Hallock:

> I can not express how...ennobling was Mr. Frelinghuysen's
> influence during the whole of his six years' presidency....In
> his addresses and in his whole life [there was such] heart-
> reaching kindness and Christian love, that I have never been
> conscious of meeting in any other man, nor do I expect ever
> to witness and enjoy it so fully again.''

The American Sunday School Union

Frelinghuysen devoted approximately thirty years of his life from 1826 into the mid-1850's to serving as vice-president of the American Sunday School Union. His early efforts were so much appreciated that he was offered the job as full-time secretary in 1836 at the handsome annual salary of $3,000. He declined but only because of his commitment to the New Jersey bar.

He worked diligently for the Union because this association was another vehicle for ''transformation.'' Spiritual conversion of youth was important to him, along with the moral effects Sunday schools had on counteracting sinful tendencies. Yet, Sunday schools for him also had a much broader educational aim: at a time when public education was in its infancy and private education was limited in the audience it served, the Sunday school emerged as ''the most benignant enterprise of modern benevolence...the fountain spring of good. In all its aspects...full of promise.''

What did it promise? A mature, democratic citizenry, came his answer. This was especially true of the frontier West where political instability was so apparent to Frelinghuysen and other leaders of the benevolent empire. The West was lawless, violent, and frequently Godless. It needed to be tamed, and the Sunday school could be an agent of such a change:

> Who would not rejoice to behold the pure spirit of religion
> pervading...our population—these sacred rules of life incul-
> cated and circulated in every valley, reaching every moun-
> taintop, and tracking every mighty river of the West?...
> Nothing besides [this] can give stability to our institutions.
> [It is true that] our Constitution is propitious to the interests
> of the Sunday school. The pure spirit of republican liberty
> invokes its aid and cherishes its fellowship, and he is
> unfaithful to his country who would impair its influence or
> check its progress.

The Sunday school, in brief, was a vanguard institution for Freling-huysen. It had a central calling to fight for political order and decency where they were so sorely lacking.

Who opposed such a program in antebellum America? The Jackson-ian Democrats, of course. It looked too Protestant and Whiggish in their eyes. Who has the most serious reservations today? Their defenders, naturally: the critics who regard the antebellum Sunday school largely as an act of conservative desperation in face of American westward expansion. Is there any truth to their charges? Perhaps. But I regard it mostly as a natural desire on the part of the Sunday school's propo-nents to help shape the future, a desire no doubt also felt by the Jackson-ians. Evangelicals probably did place too great a burden on the shoulders of the institution of the Sunday school. Although it could never have accomplished as much as it was projected to, it did provide a valuable service to the West during difficult years. And Theodore Frelinghuysen remained one of its greatest champions.

The American Temperance Union

Moral reform was endangered, Frelinghuysen believed, by the evils of liquor. The benevolent associations taking root in the American soil of the mid-1820's faced a shocking situation: "Then the land was deso-lated beyond all parallel in history....Intemperance invaded all ranks and classes. There was no place on earth so sacred that it did not assail....It depraved the public morals." Because it kept people from experiencing the total transformation called for by the organizations of benevolence, liquor had to be attacked and destroyed.

The "heaven-sent" doctrine of total abstinence was the correct solu-tion for the New Jersey statesman. He personally abstained from alco-holic beverages and supported "taking the pledge" by all Christians as a step in the right direction. He recognized, though, the necessity of additional steps. Since it was naive to expect complete success for voluntary abstinence, aggressive governmental action in the form of pro-hibition was required. Such drastic action was not an infringement on individual freedom because individuals were *not free* to harm themselves, their families and neighborhoods, or their country!

It was obviously a matter of course for a man with Frelinghuysen's leadership abilities and these convictions to assume leadership of tem-perance organizations. For many years he was the vice-president of the American Temperance Union as well as the chairman of its executive committee; he was president of the New Jersey chapter of the Ameri-can Temperance Society; and he was actively involved with efforts to reform the drinking habits of politicians in Washington, D.C. His specific efforts in this latter case are worth examining in more detail.

Senator Frelinghuysen was disturbed by what he found upon arriving in Washington, D.C., in 1829. Strong drink flowed freely (Henry Clay was one of the heaviest drinkers). Public morals were at a low ebb. Reputations suffered accordingly. He soon determined to take action. In the spring of 1832, his persistence and enthusiasm for the cause resulted in a formal meeting to discuss the possibility of launching an appropriate organization. In this effort he was supported by Senator Felix Grundy of Tennessee and Secretary of War Lewis Cass. Additional meetings followed and led to the formation of the American Congressional Temperance Society on February 26, 1833. Senator Frelinghuysen was chosen a member of the executive committee. From this position, he continued to exert a powerful witness for temperance throughout the remainder of his tenure in the Senate.

Societies for Education and Aid to the Poor

Frelinghuysen's benevolence knew few bounds. In addition to leading the societies just mentioned, he was a generous supporter of numerous agencies to aid the poor of northern New Jersey and metropolitan New York. Further, he did not limit his aid to formal institutions of charity. His nephew, Talbot Chambers, made the following observation in 1863:

> In the midst of the most exhausting period of his practice as a lawyer, it was his habit to spend every Saturday afternoon in searching out the poor and afflicted, and in ministering by sympathy as well as by pecuniary aid to their necessities, while in general he spared neither time nor means to relieve such children of sorrow as made their situation known to him.

Education too was a means to elevate the poor. Both public and private educational institutions received his gifts and encouragement. He challenged a Newark audience in 1826 to create an environment in which "not a single child in your township shall hereafter grow up in ignorance." Education was a key to democracy and prosperity "worth all the fleets that float the bosom of the ocean. It is, under Heaven, an impenetrable fortress."

The benevolent empire had virtually collapsed by the time of Frelinghuysen's death in 1862. Internal squabbling did some damage, as did the cumulative blows of denominationalism, pre-millennialism (which concentrated on other-worldly rather than this-worldly affairs), and the slavery dilemma, which helped cause the Civil War. The increasing secularism of American society also soiled the reputation of an "empire" built upon Christian principles. And I doubt whether Frelinghuysen would have been very pleased with the sporadic and ineffectual efforts at moral reformation undertaken by evangelical and Reformed Christians after the Civil War.

He was a leader of a "united front," a dynamic coalition of forces seeking a more righteous America. His leadership was characterized by his skills as public speaker, propagandist (in the positive sense), parliamentarian, committee chairman, fund raiser, and legal counselor. Few individuals in antebellum America had as many diverse gifts or the good fortune to live close to New York City, where most of the benevolent societies were headquartered. The combination produced a strong advocate in Frelinghuysen.

* * * * * * *

Questions

1. Do you think that Christian leaders want to "control" society politically more than others? If so, to what extent? If not, do you agree with the goals of the benevolent empire?

2. Would an organization like Moral Majority (Liberty Federation) be a contemporary version of the benevolent empire or any benevolent society? Why or why not? Can you name other organizations today with goals similar to those of antebellum benevolent societies?

3. To what extent is a voluntary society a good way for Christians to achieve political or social goals? Where does this leave the church? How should voluntary societies relate to the institutional church?

4. Should missions be undertaken largely through voluntary societies?

5. To what extent is leadership in the church similar to or different from leadership in voluntary societies? Should a Christian's first choice to exercise leadership gifts be in the context of the church? Explain your answer.

6. To what extent should Christian education in the Sunday school also prepare the student for citizenship?

7. Today abstinence does not seem to be a topic of high priority to most Christians. Should it be? What about abstinence and leadership, e.g., Frelinghuysen's advocacy of total abstinence? Should Christian leaders abstain from the use of alcohol as a matter of principle?

8. Is national prohibition the correct path to follow? Why or why not?

9. What were Frelinghuysen's strengths and weaknesses as a leader in relationship to benevolent societies?

10. Can you name a national figure today who is known for his/her work in the area of benevolence? What particular leadership qualities are exhibited by this individual?

11. To what extent was Frelinghuysen's leadership related to his training as a lawyer? How much does today's leadership rely on similar training?

Chapter 9

Nurturing Father

[Education] best promotes her true dignity by a cherished
sympathy with the oracles of truth. She never inflicted so
deep a wound upon all her interests, as when she strove to
put down the religion of the Bible and exalt upon its ruins
the cold speculations of infidelity.
> —Theodore Frelinghuysen, 1839

Conspicuously, through all the attributes of his character,
shone Mr. Frelinghuysen's Christian faith and devotion. No
one could spend a day in his company without being impressed with his zeal in the Master's service. His colleagues
saw that the love of Christ was the constraining principle
of his life, and it was this consistent example which rendered
his influence over the young so precious and...which...saved
them from ruin, and guided their feet in the path of
uprightness and Christian truth.
> —Howard Crosby on Frelinghuysen, 1862

The young student approached the meeting with apprehension. He
had learned with horror a few days before that a course in public speaking
was required of all incoming freshmen at New York University in the
fall of 1840. The thought of standing before his peers and displaying
his feeble attempts at oratory only dried out his mouth and raised his
normal heart rate. He had already exhausted all other avenues of appeal. Now only a direct plea to Chancellor Theodore Frelinghuysen could
save him.

He spoke as quickly and concisely as possible. He hoped he was making his point, but, just in case more was needed, he tried to entice the
chancellor with an attractive counter-proposal. If Mr. Frelinghuysen
would waive the requirement, he would double his efforts in every other department! What more could anyone ask? The chancellor was not
persuaded. "My son," he responded gently yet firmly, "no better opportunity [than such a class] would ever be offered you for the removal
of your diffidence and for the attainment of ease and readiness of
oratory."

The student, Howard Crosby, tried once again a short time later but was greeted with a similar gentle denial. Something had happened, though, by the time of the second meeting. Howard Crosby had been transformed by the gracious and loving manner in which the chancellor had conducted the two interviews and by the logic of his argument. "Instead of repelling me," Crosby later acknowledged, "these interviews won my heart, and I felt ready from that time to meet his 'my son' with a responsive 'my father.'"

Frelinghuysen's efforts in this individual's instance were handsomely rewarded. Howard Crosby went on to become an honors student in Greek and an effective public speaker during his years at New York University. At one point as a senior, he delivered a speech that was unusually well received. Descending from the stage to accept congratulations from the audience, he was greeted by the chancellor himself. With a broad, fatherly smile Frelinghuysen queried, "Are you not satisfied now that I did right in refusing you exemption from oratorical duties when you were a freshman?" Crosby could only agree—wholeheartedly.

Howard Crosby's life after graduation was one of dedicated Christian service. He became a college teacher at both New York University and Rutgers and authored numerous books and articles on Biblical studies and Christian living. He became a Presbyterian pastor, serving several prominent churches—including the Fourth Presbyterian Church of New York City. He founded the Society for the Prevention of Crime and helped organize the New York Young Men's Christian Association. At one point, he was even offered the post, which he declined, of minister to Greece by President Lincoln.

Who but perhaps a man like Theodore Frelinghuysen could have glimpsed such a future for a frightened, stammering freshman in 1840? A "freshman" who, when he first sat before the chancellor, was fourteen years old! The opportunity to nurture such a young man as Howard Crosby was one of the principal reasons why Frelinghuysen left the bar and politics in the late 1830's to pursue a career in education. He had always loved students and regarded education as a high Christian calling.

He had also grown somewhat weary of politics and the heavy duties of the bar. He would never completely abandon politics: note his 1844 campaign as chancellor for the vice-presidency. By the late 1830's, nonetheless, he was frustrated with his inability to accomplish more politically. Part of this frustration can easily be seen in his 1838 book, written while he was dealing as mayor with the difficult problems of funding a rapidly growing city like Newark at a time of economic recession. Perhaps, he thought, education would be more productive and more restful. Being "restful" was also important because his health had deteriorated under the weight of his many responsibilities. (Chambers spoke of his "disordered nerves.")

Frelinghuysen was thus happy to hear the news early in 1839 of his unanimous selection by the New York University council as chancellor. From the point of view of the university, it was a logical choice. According to Chamberlain, "[Frelinghuysen] was chosen because it was desired to place at the head of the institution a man of character so eminent in consistency of Christian virtues, combined with wide and honorable experience in public career, as to endow the...College with a prestige derivable from no other source." From Frelinghuysen's perspective, the choice was made easier because he envisioned university life to be more serene and because he had been led to believe that his ascension to the chancellorship would bring considerably more money into the university. Neither hope, as we shall see, would be completely realized.

How did others respond to the statesman's shift from politics to education? Mostly, it seems, with enthusiasm. Christians especially were delighted to see one of their own assume leadership of a major university. Yet, a few dissenting voices were heard. Several lawyers, in particular, were reluctant to see him leave the bar where "his particular gifts, his quick insight, his sharp discrimination, his impetuous eloquence, shone with greatest lustre." One fellow attorney even claimed that putting him in charge of a university was "like burying him in a marble mausoleum before his time had come."

New York University

Although neither the U.S. Senate nor the New Jersey bar, New York University was hardly a mausoleum. In 1839 it was a university with great promise located in the major urban center in America. The council hoped that with the right leadership and with an expanding constituency it would grow to rival the best of the Ivy League colleges and universities. No doubt they shared this dream with their new executive.

Frelinghuysen served as chancellor for eleven years. These were years of growth and development in the university as well as of disappointment. One positive sign was the increase in the number of students attending the university, an increase particularly impressive in the late 1830's and early 1840's when the effects of the economic recession were still evident. I would attribute this growth in part to the natural appeal of Frelinghuysen's name to the large Christian market. Another positive development in the university was the improved quality of the faculty under Frelinghuysen, led by the noted churchman, Dr. C.F. Henry. The faculty was particularly strong during those years in Latin, German, theology, and Oriental studies. It was also truly ecumenical, representing the Presbyterian, Episcopalian, and Dutch Reformed denominations, among others. All evidence points to the fact that Frelinghuysen took great pride in the quality and catholicity of his faculty and gave faculty recruitment high priority.

Finally, the physical structure of the university developed during

Frelinghuysen's tenure in office, if only slightly. Most of the actual growth was related to the founding of the university's medical college. Although begun in 1838, the facilities (as well as curriculum and faculty) were expanded during the first months and years of Frelinghuysen's chancellorship. He was, as we might expect, very proud of the medical school and anticipated that its graduates would provide great service to the community.

On the other hand, two situations made life especially burdensome for Chancellor Frelinghuysen. The first involved a struggle between the chancellor and one individual who opposed his administration. According to Chamberlain's account, this opponent, apparently a faculty or council member, attacked the chancellor's every decision, carrying on a virtual vendetta against Frelinghuysen's leadership. There is no indication that Frelinghuysen responded in kind, or made any public acknowledgement of his adversary, but it surely must have been an emotionally draining experience for him. Hardly the pastoral environment he had coveted when departing the battleground of politics!

Financial troubles, though, proved to be Frelinghuysen's greatest frustration. He was aware of the university's large debt when he accepted his position, but he hoped, as did the council and many of his Christian friends, that his ascension to the chancellorship would be a turning of the corner financially. And some progress was made. Some of the debt was retired during the 1840's. The overall picture, however, continued to be a discouraging one.

Two factors created much of the financial dilemma. One was a fire which had taken place just prior to Frelinghuysen's arrival. The fire caused considerable damage to buildings, requiring extra fund raising at a time of economic uncertainty. The second discouraging note occurred in the mid-1840's when New York State withdrew most of its financial support from New York University. The university had depended upon the good graces of the legislature during the 1830's and found withdrawal a difficult problem to deal with. How was the university to compensate for the loss of such necessary funds? This question plagued Frelinghuysen during the last years and months of his administration.

In the final analysis, it was no doubt the financial situation which drove Frelinghuysen away from New York University in 1850. At the age of sixty-three, he no longer had the physical or emotional strength to undertake all the duties of the chancellorship in addition to bearing the financial burden. Other incentives, however, were also operating to lure him back across the Hudson River toward the friendly shores of New Jersey.

Rutgers College

Rutgers College seemed to Frelinghuysen the perfect place to finish his public career. It was the college of his ancestral denomination, the

Dutch Reformed Church. It was also a college with whom he had family connections. Rutgers had been born a few years before the American Revolution (in 1770) as Queen's College, thanks to the fatherly efforts of its first president, Jacobus Hardenberg. Rev. Hardenberg, as you recall, was the second husband of Theodore's beloved grandmother, Dinah. During the early 1800's it had fallen on hard times, only to be reborn (and renamed) in 1825. Having the opportunity in 1850, as New Jersey's "favorite son," to serve as the third president of the new era, filled Frelinghuysen's heart with great peace and gratitude.

Frelinghuysen worked diligently to live up to the faith in him evidenced by the unanimous choice and high praise of the Rutgers' board of trustees. Although hardly plush, Rutgers' finances were in better shape than New York University's at the moment of Frelinghuysen's acceptance of the presidency. This relative security did not, though, keep him from devoting considerable time and effort to fund raising, especially within his ancestral church. His fund-raising letters were filled with urgent appeals to give to "the only college of our Dutch Church—a church dear to our forefathers and dear to you and me." Such appeals were largely successful. During his tenure, a large portion of Rutgers' debt was retired and the endowment significantly increased.

The Rutgers' student body increased steadily during the Frelinghuysen years. Only the Civil War would halt the expansion. That quality as well as quantity characterized these years can be seen by the following list, from Demarest's study, of students who graduated under Frelinghuysen's presidency, subsequently to leave their mark upon society: John Bogard ('53)—"the greatest physician of his generation"; Edward G. Janeway ('60)—"the greatest celestial mathematician in the world of his day"; and George William Hill ('59)—a natural scientist, Rutgers' "greatest product" who could only be called a "genius." Not all students, of course, were of this caliber, but whatever their abilities and potential, President Frelinghuysen took enormous pride in them.

Upon assuming the presidency in 1850, Frelinghuysen also became professor of international and constitutional law and moral philosophy. Professor Frelinghuysen joined an already prestigious faculty, most notable of whom were Dr. Theodore Strong (mathematics), Dr. Lewis C. Beck (chemistry), and the venerable Dr. James S. Cannon (metaphysics). Frelinghuysen worked to maintain such a highly qualified faculty during his tenure at Rutgers. Thanks in part to his efforts, three outstanding new teachers were added: Rev. Dr. William H. Campbell (literature), Rev. Dr. John Ludlow (metaphysics), and Professor George H. Cook (chemistry and the natural sciences). Demarest amply documents the various contributions of these three teachers in his book on the history of Rutgers College.

The curriculum at Rutgers remained quite traditional. The primary academic focus continued to be mathematics and the natural sciences, the classics, Hebrew and Greek, and philosophy. Such courses as modern languages, physical education, and even specific study of English language and literature were neglected or in their infancy. It appears that President Frelinghuysen was relatively content with the more traditional curriculum.

The physical plant remained largely the same, with one outstanding exception: the construction of a new theological building. Frelinghuysen and others had become convinced that the college and the Reformed seminary should be physically separated. Both institutions had utilized Queen's building since the college was revived in 1825, but this cooperation proved unworkable by the mid-1850's; there was simply no more room with which to expand. Someone had to move, and the seminary took the initiative. Frelinghuysen made his plea for funds to a respected widow, Mrs. Ann Hertzog; she consented, making a generous gift of $30,000 as a memorial to her husband, Peter Hertzog. A site was chosen a few hundred feet north of the campus. On November 8, 1855, the cornerstone was laid for the Peter Hertzog Theological Hall; the finished building was dedicated on September 23, 1856. According to Demarest, it was "an imposing, spacious building, providing lecture rooms and library and chapel, besides living rooms and dining rooms for students." No one was more delighted with this "altogether attractive" building and surroundings than President Frelinghuysen.

In sum, Frelinghuysen enjoyed his twilight years as president of Rutgers. No internal enemies surfaced, the students "revered" him, and the New Brunswick community responded warmly to his presence. Further, many different tasks appealed to him as an educational leader: chairing faculty meetings, soliciting funds, recruiting faculty and students, and teaching. He seemed to thrive on all this work. In fact, his health actually improved; no longer were his nerves frayed by either the strains of politics or the disappointments of his later years at New York University. He was finally "at home" as President Frelinghuysen.

In light of the foregoing, I would judge that he was relatively successful as an educational leader. But more needs to be said. What about his leadership style and his philosophy of education? And what, if any, weaknesses in his leadership capabilities existed?"

Leadership: Style and Philosophy

Two possible weaknesses in the character of the leadership need to be mentioned. The first involved the substantial amount of work Frelinghuysen undertook. Few college presidents today would try to accomplish as much, would attempt to be involved in so many different kinds of activities. But Frelinghuysen could be criticized for attempting too much and as a result spreading himself too thinly, especially when seen in the light of his other Kingdom activities—like providing direction for the benevolent empire. This is one reason why I judge his leadership as "relatively" successful. In no one area was he preeminently triumphant.

Possibly a second weakness can be seen in his attitude toward leadership. Was he appropriately aggressive and purposeful as he made decisions and delegated authority? Did his attitude and resulting actions reflect a "commanding presence" as an educational leader? To answer these questions, I will draw upon the testimony of Dr. Tayler Lewis, who for many years served as a colleague of Frelinghuysen. (Although this relationship developed at New York University, I judge the evaluation would be equally true of Rutgers.)

Dr. Lewis had high hopes in 1839 that Chancellor Frelinghuysen would "take the lead commandingly" as the new pilot of New York University. Such was the approach he expected from a former senator who had recently confronted President Jackson on the BUS and Indian rights issues. But Lewis' hopes were not to be fulfilled, at least not as he had anticipated. For him, Frelinghuysen's whole approach to educational leadership was disappointing:

> It was not the commanding character imagination had pictured....it was, indeed, a fault in this great man and this pure Christian that he had a way of so constantly deferring to others. It was the carrying to excess of the apostle's precept: "Let each man esteem others better than himself"....he sat in our midst...as one who sought to learn from others rather than command, and who would substitute [the faculty's] professional knowledge for his own wide and catholic experience.

Deference was the central problem. Frelinghuysen tried too hard to placate his faculty, to smooth over the ruffled feathers of faculty and council, so much so that too much of his own initiative was taken away from him; in brief, he often appeared to Lewis to be following rather than assertively leading.

This was Lewis' appraisal upon first acquaintance with Chancellor Frelinghuysen. Later on a different picture emerged. Lewis came to love the very signs of deference and humility which he had previously criticized. Poignantly, he came to describe Frelinghuysen as one who

> imparted strength, but not as I had expected. He was an admirable illustration of the apostle's paradox: "When he was weak, then he was strong;" and "out of his weakness" were made strong those who enjoyed the privilege of this blessed Christian intercommunion [with him]....His whole soul was in the pilgrimage to the New Jerusalem....he was a *"seeker of salvation"*....His mind was ever upon his demerits, his deficiencies. It was no mock humility....He

was a very humble man, and in this lies the very essence
of his greatness and his strength.

What a remarkable transformation in just a few years of Lewis' evaluation of the same man. But the second picture is not entirely satisfying.
The simple fact remains that leaders must *lead*. They are called to do
it Christianly, i.e., normatively, but they must lead, nonetheless. Constantly deferring to the opinion of others can be more than a sign of
true Christian humility. It can also be a sign of weakness. Perhaps more
development could have occurred at both institutions if Frelinghuysen
had been more specialized in his interests and more assertive in the style
of his leadership.

I have more sympathy for Frelinghuysen's philosophy of education,
which can be expressed in six related propositions:

1. "Education is a truly academic-intellectual exercise." Faithful to
his Reformed heritage, Frelinghuysen took a strong stand against the
anti-intellectualism emanating from some of his contemporary evangelical
cousins. Education, he declared in his 1839 inaugural,

> is designed to lead the mind into the proper use of its pow-
> ers...to teach it how to think and how to learn. Like the
> apprenticeship of the mechanic, who should first be taught
> the nature and use of his tools, so the student must first learn
> the nature of the faculties which God has bestowed and the
> way by which he is to bring them into exercise.

"We have at last come to the full acknowledgement of what...we were
slow to learn," he reiterated in his 1850 inaugural, "that...God has
endowed man with immortal [mental] faculties, capable of indefinite
improvement." In the proper exercise of these faculties, we become
truly educated men, and educated men are a "public blessing."

2. "Education is more than reason alone." Despite his acknowledgement of the importance of the intellect, Frelinghuysen always recognized its limitations. It was not education which saved us, not our own
minds which first brought us to our knees before God. Speaking on the
theme of education before a Christian audience as early as 1826, he
concluded:

> I come not to exalt the reign of reason. Her only safe posture
> is that of an humble learner, in a better school. I speak to
> a Christian people, who feel that all this intellectual cultiva-
> tion reaches not the heart, and that still the sage, equally with
> the savage, needs the energy of Divine Grace, to quicken
> the soul from its spiritual death.

Frelinghuysen quickly reminded this same audience that education was
important; reason did clarify difficult issues and restrain our passions,
but it was of secondary spiritual significance. It was the product of grace,

not the producer.

Howard Crosby recalled how Frelinghuysen's greatest delight came not from classroom teaching but from his regular habit of exhorting students in chapel from the Word. In fact, the high point of Frelinghuysen's day came when he could implore students to live "a godly life." Such a life was more than reason alone could supply.

3. "Education is holistic." Proper Biblical education, for Frelinghuysen, was holistic—involving the emotional as well as the spiritual and mental sides of reality. He knew from personal experience how important emotional health was to the learning process.

4. "Education reveals God." All of the curriculum, not just the humanities and theology, revealed God and His handiwork, declared Frelinghuysen. Thus science and the Bible were not enemies but allies. "The whole circle of the natural sciences," he proclaimed in his 1850 inaugural address, "tends to confirm the revelations of the Scriptures and demonstrate that the Author of nature is the God of the Bible." He concluded: "One great truth stands out in prominence, as the tribute of all sound philosophy. That the intelligence, skill and counsels, of the Infinite and Glorious Creator, may be clearly traced, and shine forth illustriously in the work of His power; in the worlds of matter, as of mind." Christian education would compel students to see that God is "the cause of causes."

5. "Teachers are the moral guardians of students." College teachers, Frelinghuysen believed, had moral responsibility for their students. In fact, the protective relationship between teacher and student was one of *in loco parentis* (in place of the parents): "These guardians," he noted in the 1850 address, "are clothed with authority, that is essentially parental—because they are entrusted to mould the habits and to restrain the waywardness of the sons—to give the right direction to thought and intention." Once teachers forgot this imperative, Christian education was truly imperiled.

6. "Meeting God: the ultimate goal of education." Here, Frelinghuysen reformulated point two, but with a different slant. Here, the teacher became the evangelist, for in the final analysis a transformed life was the goal of education. And only a confrontation with the living God could bring this about. "And beyond and above all," he implored a student, Thomas King, in 1844, "give all diligence to secure the one thing needful in life, the favor of God and the love of the Savior." Why such an emphasis? Because Frelinghuysen believed, as Crosby noted, that "the student was, first of all, a sinner requiring the atoning blood of Jesus, and all learning and discipline were subordinate...to the great end of spiritual conversion and renewal."

What conclusions can we draw from these six educational principles? First, on the positive side, they are balanced, Reformed, and evangelical. Frelinghuysen correctly envisioned that college education was a blending of different dimensions of life, that it was to glorify God, and that bringing the student into a personal relationship with the Author of knowledge was its loftiest goal. Surely we need to be reminded of these truths today.

Second, I would raise only one objection, relating to point five. Teachers do resemble parents in some ways. They have a kind of authority over students and should develop a caring and loving relationship with them. The *in loco parentis* principle, however, misconstrues the relationship and is not generally accepted today. The teacher-student relationship is qualitatively different than the parent-child one. In the former, the submission is voluntary and based on the teacher's possession of a special kind of theoretical knowledge. It is the sharing of this knowledge among adults, including the art of critical thinking, which distinguishes college education from parental nurturing. The ethical relationship of teacher and student should always be seen in this context. Consequently, the teacher is much less the moral "guardian" and much more the moral "companion," teachers and students together seeking to understand the moral principles of God's Word and world. In advocating *in loco parentis,* the older view, Frelinghuysen was more a creature of his age than a progressive thinker.

In conclusion, I am impressed with the overall "spiritual" thrust of Frelinghuysen's later life. He increasingly directed his lectures, letters, conversations, and chapel talks to the deeper, spiritual truths of Christianity. I attribute this in part to a natural aging process, a road traveled by many Christians as they mature and face death. But it was more pronounced in Frelinghuysen than in most believers. And it was consistent with his lifelong burden for the souls of men. Above all else, he was always willing and prepared to witness to others. The remarkable extent of his personal evangelism will be the focus of the next chapter.

* * * * * * *

Discussion Questions

1. What leadership qualities did Frelinghuysen manifest in his relationship with Howard Crosby, the student mentioned at the beginning of the chapter?

2. In 1839 Frelinghuysen made a major vocational shift, from law and politics to education. Was it a wise move? Was it a mistake for him to "imprison" himself in a "marble mausoleum"? Can you name a leader today who has made a similar move or a move from politics to another profession other than education?

3. Would you agree with my judgment that Frelinghuysen was only relatively successful as an educational leader? Why or why not?

4. I've praised the quality of students and faculty at both New York

University and Rutgers during the Frelinghuysen years. To what extent was this quality a sign of leadership?

5. Frelinghuysen took great pride in the construction of Hertzog Theological Hall at Rutgers. How would you relate this development to the overall characterization of his leadership?

6. I've suggested that as an educational leader at both institutions Frelinghuysen was spread too thinly, i.e., he tried to do too much. How does a leader (or a community) know when "too much" is being attempted or expected?

7. Which is more important for a leader, "commanding presence" or "humility"? Or is it a combination of both? Can you name a Christian leader today who has successfully combined these traits?

8. What do you think of Frelinghuysen's philosophy of education as expressed in the six principles? Do you agree with my criticism of *in loco parentis*? Why or why not?

9. What should be the primary concern of a Christian educational leader?

10. To what extent are the traits necessary for successful educational leadership similar to those of political leadership?

Chapter 10

Full-time Evangelist

He wanted Christ to be on the throne, and all men at His footstool, doing the divine will and enjoying the divine blessing.

—W.H. Campbell on Frelinghuysen, 1862

Mr. Frelinghuysen seemed never to lose an opportunity [for evangelism]. His heart was so burdened with concern for all out of Christ, that he has been known more than once, after passing unconverted persons in the street, to be constrained by his own painful emotions to turn back and speak with them on the state of their souls.

—Talbot Chambers, 1862

Vain is the help of man, and frail and fatal all trust in the arm of flesh; but he that trusteth in the Lord shall be as Mount Zion itself, that can never be removed.

—Frelinghuysen to Henry Clay, 1844

It was April, 1862, and Theodore Frelinghuysen lay on his deathbed. He was physically weak and failing rapidly. Family and friends remained close to him, paying what they suspected would be their "last respects." Tears of grief and Christian hope flowed freely: death would be sad but eternal life beckoned him.

A day or two before his death, Theodore's close friend and soon-to-be successor at Rutgers, Dr. W.H. Campbell, visited him. Dr. Campbell, holding Theodore's hand, bade him goodbye: "Farewell, Mr. Frelinghuysen, farewell. I expect soon to join you. I shall not long remain here. Farewell, sir." President Frelinghuysen summoned enough strength to reply, "Farewell, my friend, but you must stay here. God has a work for you, and you will yet accomplish great good." Campbell did accomplish much good in subsequent years, and, amazingly, so did Frelinghuysen—even in the short time remaining to him.

Just hours before his death, Frelinghuysen welcomed into his room a youth of about seventeen, a son of a close friend. The dying president longed to speak with this young man about salvation because he suspected that the youth had never committed his life to Jesus as Savior and Lord. Perhaps, he thought, his own testimony and death would be used by God to reach this youth's heart.

> I have sent for you, my son. I want you to see how a Christian can die. I have been all my life in fear of that hour, and yet [recently] I have seen death day by day approaching, and never was calmer. Did you ever see me more calm? [Receiving a negative reply he continued.] Now, my son, do not despise parents' prayers, mothers' tears, and sisters' supplications, but turn to God. Now is the accepted time, now is the day of salvation. Seek the Lord, and you will find him....He has not come away from heaven and died upon earth to be lightly rejected.

To encourage the youth further, Frelinghuysen presented him with a special gift, a Bible from the American Bible Society. He urged the young man to make daily Bible reading a habit. This would confront him with the gospel and, once a decision had been made, draw him near to his Savior and strengthen his faith. "My son, farewell," whispered Frelinghuysen. "Go now, and seek God's grace."

The manner in which this tale was recounted by Talbot Chambers seems to suggest that the young man did commit his life to Christ. Whether he did or not, though, it accurately reflects Frelinghuysen's dedication to full-time evangelism. Once his own reluctance to speak to others about Christ had been overcome by his 1820 "conversion" following the death of his brother, Theodore witnessed to others whenever and wherever he could. According to Chambers, "All times and places, all ages and sexes were alike to him in this respect. He had the heart to bear witness for Christ, and by God's grace he found the way." His style of witnessing, as noted by friends, was "judicious and unobtrusive," thoroughly winsome in every respect. As a result, he led many individuals to Christ—from all walks of life, as we shall see.

He was able to assume the role of "Mr. Layman" in terms of successful evangelism because of the depth of his theology, a theology which led him to reject the tendency among some conservative laymen to withdraw from soul winning in deference to the clergy. In 1855 he summarized his perspective in the following manner:

> [F]or the more solemn duties of the sanctuary and its worship, and for the governance and order of Christ's Church, the ministers are to "be called" and set apart, yet for exhortation, and prayer, and witnessing for the truth, and warning sinners, and encouraging the trembling believer, we are all to labor for Christ, and have a heart and a tongue for his blessed service.

Obviously, no false dualism relegating evangelistic work to the clergy only was possible for someone holding such a stance. Evangelism was everyone's responsibility.

What follows in the next pages are just a few examples of the nature and extent of Frelinghuysen's evangelism.

Students: A Typical Example

Howard Crosby, Tayler Lewis, and many others all commented on Frelinghuysen's lifelong concern for the spiritual welfare of students. One of the best examples of this concern can be seen from a series of fifteen letters written by Senator Frelinghuysen to an unnamed student between 1829 and 1835. Although he is unnamed, it is clear that they were addressed to one of his nephews.

On the surface, the subject of all the letters was education, since the student had launched his educational career in 1829, at the same time that Frelinghuysen had journeyed to Washington, D.C. "Uncle" Theodore thus encouraged the novice to establish his future upon "solid learning," to strive to become an "accomplished scholar," and to master a useful profession (apparently law). Throughout the correspondence, Frelinghuysen rejoiced in the student's academic efforts:

> I am happy to learn from your letters that you are at hard study. I know that it is wholesome. The brain needs action. It is like flint—to have fire you must strike it....If you wish to give it [the mind] strength, and tone, and compass, you must put its powers to the trial, bring them out to stern, severe, and laborious exercise.

Yet, education was only a minor theme in the correspondence. The second and more crucial message was a spiritual one. Every letter, in fact, led from education to religion, for Frelinghuysen knew that the student had never turned his life over to Christ! The following statements—each taken from a different letter—exemplify Frelinghuysen's major theme:

> My dear _____, realize that you are a sinner, that you need a Savior, and that whatever else you may gain, if you do not secure an interest in the mercy of God through the blood of His dear Son, you will be an everlasting victim of His wrath.

> You say nothing of the state of your feelings on the most important of all subjects—how you stand affected toward your Creator....He has claims, my dear child, which cannot be disregarded without great danger and guilt.

> I beg you to be concerned at the condition in which you stand before [God]. He is waiting to be gracious. He points you to the blood of His Son as your refuge. He calls, invites,

95

and commands you to turn unto Him and live—to repent and
believe, and be saved, or perish.

> There is a dearer wish that I cherish for you [than educa-
> tional success]: that you may turn away from the vain show
> of this perishing world, and place your affections on Him
> whose you are, and whom you are bound to love and serve.
> This, my dear _____, is the highest wisdom.

Theodore's prayers and efforts were apparently successful, for in the
last few letters a new note of optimism appeared. On December 17,
1834, he wrote, "I am rejoiced to learn that you feel a measure of your
own foulness as well as guilt....Bless the Lord that he has given you
any sense of your character and condition, and led you to feel at all
your need of a Savior." And on January 13, 1835, he could celebrate
because "the Lord has led you by His Spirit....out of nature's darkness
from the reigning power of sin to the love of His blessed and holy character, law, and service." Talbot Chambers at one point suggested that
Frelinghuysen's witnessing was always persistent but not always successful. Obviously the correspondence with his nephew just described
is an example of persistence and success.

William Pennington

→William Pennington was a powerful political figure in New Jersey
and in the nation. He was a successful attorney, a member of the state
Assembly, and New Jersey's governor for six one-year terms. He was
offered, but declined, posts as governor of the Minnesota territory and
as claims judge under the Mexican (war) treaty of 1848. He was also
a man of sincere religious convictions, concerning which he made the
following confession in an April, 1858, letter written to Frelinghuysen:

> And it is due from me to say that I ascribe much of my rever-
> ence for divine things, and, indeed, my strongest and firm-
> est religious impressions, to your [Frelinghuysen's] advice
> and example—the living example, that is the preacher, after
> all, with the conscience and the intellect....I confide in the
> promises, and in the hope that I have made a full and hum-
> ble surrender penitently to the blessed Redeemer of the
> world.

From this quote it is clear that Theodore Frelinghuysen was Pennington's spiritual mentor, his conversion and religious worldview due in
large part to the ministrations of the Christian statesman. Such an
influence should come as no surprise, for Pennington studied law under Frelinghuysen, became his ally in Whig politics, and supported
Frelinghuysen's educational leadership. Such a spiritual influence had
its effect in the public arena as well as in Pennington's private life, for,

a few months after writing the above letter, William Pennington was elected to Congress from New Jersey and was chosen speaker of the U.S. House of Representatives!

Ezekiel F. Chambers

→Ezekiel Chambers was a prominent Maryland political figure whose background was similar to Pennington's. An attorney who began his political career in the Maryland Senate in 1822, he was appointed in 1826 to the U.S. Senate and served through 1834—thus making him a colleague of Frelinghuysen. In 1834 he left politics to accept an appointed position as chief judge of Maryland's second judicial district and judge of the state's court of appeals. President Millard Fillmore offered him the position of secretary of the navy in 1852, but he declined because of ill health. Finally, Chambers served as a member of the 1850 and 1864 Maryland state conventions, called to write new constitutions.

Like Pennington, Chambers' spiritual life was indebted to Theodore Frelinghuysen. His appreciation is evident in the following letter, written in March, 1854:

> I have never ceased to have a warm regard [for Theodore Frelinghuysen]; whose kind, considerate, and Christian counsel has been willingly tendered when impatience of spirit...would mislead me, and whose amiable and disinterested aid was never withheld when needed....It will afford me great pleasure to see you once more before one or the other shall be called away; but, if not on earth, I humbly trust we may in heaven renew our greetings.

James S. Nevius

→James Nevius was another distinguished member of the New Jersey bar. He also served for several years on the state Supreme Court. Frelinghuysen witnessed to him for many years about the need for personal commitment to the living Christ. Nevius had for some time been on the brink of a decision when this letter arrived from his "evangelist" friend:

> It seems to me, after much reflection on the terms of your letter, that the only hindrance in your way is in the unwillingness of your heart to give up all its pleas and strivings... and to fall down a poor, lost, wretched sinner at the Savior's feet....Here it is—believe it: there is no obstacle but in a proud heart that will not bow down all the way to dust and ashes before God, and exclaim, "O Lord! I surrender." ...For who is this gracious Redeemer? Remember that He is God manifest in the flesh....now all He asks of you is,

"Son, give me thine heart," and you have refused Him this small tribute for years and years....Submit now, unreservedly, and all will be peace.

A few weeks after receiving this letter, according to Talbot Chambers, James Nevius surrendered his life to Christ!

Daniel Webster

→Frelinghuysen did not hesitate, either, to reach out to those actors who were "giants" on the American political stage, stars like Daniel Webster. No evidence exists that he was successful in converting Webster, but he did try. The two men shared a Whig platform on several occasions and were friends who carried on a cordial correspondence. In 1848 Webster suffered the loss of a loved one. Frelinghuysen wrote a letter of condolence which received the following reply from Webster; Frelinghuysen's evangelical message can easily be inferred:

In the midst of severe affliction, my dear friend, I hear your voice tendering...sympathy...I feel that nothing else is left, and I pray God that I may receive the chastening with a penitent and believing heart. It is not for me to say whether He shall call me or my children first into His presence. I know that there we must all shortly appear....the sun of our lives is fast going down; my own, especially, is near the horizon. I [do] wish to consider all things earthly as held by a precious tie, and by that tie still more precious I am held to those who love me.

Henry Clay

Frelinghuysen's admiration for Henry Clay has been previously noted. The Christian statesman considered the Kentuckian to be America's leading politician, eminently qualified to be president. He was a devoted disciple of Clay's American system and felt that it alone was the solution to America's political ills. Clay, however, remained throughout his life on the fringe of the Christian community, apparently never experiencing an evangelical "conversion" to Christ, though he did join the Episcopal Church in 1847, five years before his death. Clay's reluctance was a source of great disappointment to Frelinghuysen. He wanted nothing as much as the salvation of Henry Clay.

This heartfelt desire was evident throughout Frelinghuysen's lifelong correspondence with Clay. I find their letters to be quite astonishing. Frelinghuysen always found a means of directing the subject of each letter to Clay's spiritual life, or better, to his lack of true spirituality. It did not phase him at all that he was speaking to one of the most powerful men in American politics. In his mind Clay, it seems, was just like everyone else: a sinner in need of a Savior.

We can see the evangelist at work in just a few excerpts from their mutual correspondence.

1. Late in 1835, Frelinghuysen consoled Clay on the death of a favorite daughter. Although his letter hasn't survived, we can infer much from Clay's response of January 16, 1836:

> But I thank you, my dear friend, still more for the deep interest which you so kindly take in my spiritual welfare. I should be most happy to have the confidence and assurance which you feel on that serious subject. It is one on which...I have [given] long and great...solicitude...and I indulge the hope that I shall ultimately find the peace which you have attained.

2. On May 11, 1844, Frelinghuysen wrote how pleased he was to be nominated as vice-president on the Whig ticket. It was for him a "rich political privilege" to be associated with a man of Clay's stature. Then, in the same paragraph, he quite calmly stated, "My prayer for you and my own soul shall be fervent that, through the rich grace of our Savior, [our names] may be found written in the Book of Life of the Lamb that was slain for our sins."

After November's narrow defeat—so bitter to Clay—Frelinghuysen wrote a letter of sympathy, blaming the loss on the stridency of the abolitionists and the block voting of immigrants. He then casually shifted gears:

> But, my dear sir, leaving this painful subject, let us look away to brighter and better prospects...in the promises...of the Gospel of our Savior. As sinners who have rebelled against our Maker, we need a Savior or we must perish, and this Redeemer has been provided us...."Come unto me," cries this exalted Savior....Let us then repair to Him. He will never fail us in the hour of peril and trial....I pray, my honored friend, that your heart may seek this blessed refuge....

Clay responded openly a few days later:

> You have, my dear friend...kindly suggested the truest of all consolations in the resources of our holy religion. I have long been persuaded of that solemn truth; nor have I been entirely neglectful of exertions to secure to myself its benefits. I wish I could add that I feel entire confidence that these exertions had been crowned with success....I trust that, by diligent searching, I shall find, in faith in our Lord Jesus, that solace which no earthly honors or possession can give

3. In response to a letter from Frelinghuysen in 1846, Clay confessed that he had been regularly attending services in the Episcopal Church, but "I must own, however, with regret, that I do not feel that absolute

confidence in my future salvation which some Christians profess to have in theirs."

4. Upon hearing of Clay's illness in 1852, Frelinghuysen made one last missionary effort:

> In this time of impaired health....it must be refreshing to look away to Him who is a helper near in trouble....This blessed Gospel...is a wonderful remedy...so full of inexpressible consolation to us as sinners needing mercy, His blood cleansing us from the guilt of sin....May you, my dear friend, largely partake of its comforts, and leaning all our hopes on the Almighty Savior's arm, hold on...for life and death, for time and eternity [to] His name and strength.

Clay died on June 29, 1852. Frelinghuysen wrote his eulogy for the *New York Times* a few days later. In it, he could only express his fondest hope that his friend had indeed made his peace with God through the blood of Christ. He then pointed to Clay's lifelong search for salvation. "Religion," he said, "was no new subject for his last sickness. [Clay] had anxiously and deeply meditated [throughout his life] on this high concern for the soul's salvation." Perhaps, concluded Frelinghuysen, the calm and peaceful manner of Clay's death was proof of his final destiny. Perhaps.

In an earlier chapter I hinted at the possibility of some tension between these two vital figures, an uneasiness based on latent political jealousy. Evidence for such a tension could be inferred in light of the material in this chapter. I can't quite get over the impression that Frelinghuysen's letters were sincere but Clay's merely "cordial." Was Clay offended by Frelinghuysen's frankness? Was Frelinghuysen's approach presumptuous or even audacious to Clay or does it only seem to be to our somewhat jaded modern ears? Was Clay, therefore, just going through the motions in terms of polite responses to Frelinghuysen's persistent evangelism? How else could a sophisticated man like Clay respond to such a constant barrage of evangelical missiles from a political ally, except politely? Maybe in his final years Clay did become more religious; his membership in the Episcopal Church might be evidence of sincerity. But the literature on the younger man, the dashing ladies' man who loved dueling and gambling, hardly seems an appropriate model for a "pilgrim's progress." If I'm correct, we have all the more reason to be impressed with Theodore's lengthy trolling for the soul of this particular sinner.

Conclusion

There are four ways, I believe, in which Frelinghuysen's soul-winning can be seen as normative for us today. First, it was extensive, broad in scope, leaving no one outside its purview. Frelinghuysen was concerned about the spiritual condition of all individuals—young and old, women and men, students and professors, the high as well as the low. Second, it was fearless, for the "high," as we have seen, were the regional and national political leaders of his age. He did not hesitate to speak to them, either, about their need for a Savior. I've mentioned only a few in this category; numerous others also felt his outstretched hand. Third, it was persistent. He did not give up easily; in fact, it appears that he never gave up. His correspondence with Henry Clay, for example, covered nearly twenty years. Fourth, it was inescapable. Frelinghuysen realized that whatever a man's calling in life, whatever his situation, all Christians were obliged to give an account of their faith when an opportunity presented itself. The joy of evangelism ought to be shared by all!

If there was any weakness in Frelinghuysen's approach, it might be a tendency to over-spiritualize his written communication. He, of course, had firsthand knowledge of each context, but I sometimes feel that he was being a little emotionally manipulative in his letters. Sometimes he appeared to discuss the events or crises in any area as if there were always a direct link between that area and an individual's spiritual life or lack of it. Maybe there always is. But there are also times, for example, when a student's educational problem is fundamentally academic in nature. In other words, his "spirit" is low because he is not applying himself academically, not because his spiritual life is in disarray. Not all problems are religious in the sense of being only problems of the "heart."

* * * * * * *

Discussion Questions

1. To what extent can a Christian politician or educational leader be a full-time evangelist? What conflicts, tensions, or problems might such a leader encounter if he also engages in evangelism? What is the role of the layman in evangelism?

2. I've suggested that Frelinghuysen tended to stress the primacy of conversion in his voluminous correspondence. Are there any dangers in this attitude? Was he manipulative?

3. What does Frelinghuysen's relationship to Pennington, Chambers, and Nevius say about his style of leadership?

4. What is the appropriate stance of a Christian in terms of the evangelization of prominent national leaders? How can we reach them? How should Christian politicians relate to their nonbelieving colleagues?

5. What does Frelinghuysen's correspondence with Henry Clay say about his style of leadership? Was he manipulative with Clay?

6. Is it possible that Clay was offended by Frelinghuysen's approach? Would Frelinghuysen's style be acceptable in today's political world? Why or why not?

7. What limits would you suggest to evangelistic persistence? Should we ever give up? When?

8. Can you name some Christian leaders today outside of the church or evangelistic organizations who have Frelinghuysen's passion for souls? What is their style of witnessing?

Chapter 11

Heart, Home, And Sanctuary

This, I think, doctor, is my last struggle; and it is all peace—
Christ is precious....Christ has opened me to the truth. If
there had been no sin, we should not have known how gracious God is.
        —Theodore Frelinghuysen on his deathbed, 1862

Theodore Frelinghuysen was the gift of God to the American people. [He was] a bright and shining example of the
thorough and consistent Christian in all walks of life, public and private.
        —A friend, 1862

The seventeen-year-old youth to whom Frelinghuysen witnessed on
his deathbed also heard a very unusual confession from the venerated
leader, namely, that an abject fear of death had plagued him throughout his life. Few individuals had been privileged with such information; only his wife and closest friends ever knew of his deepest doubts.
Why, we are compelled to ask, did this man of God question his own
faith and for so long? That it was a problem for him comes from the
first-hand testimony of friends attending his last days on earth. The testimony that follows doesn't give an answer to the *why?* only to the fact
that it existed.

The problem, in a nutshell, can be glimpsed in a brief encounter with
one of his nieces during his final winter, 1861-62. "Ah! it is a solemn
thing to be so near eternity," he greeted her one morning as she entered his room to nurse him. "We indeed feel that," she replied, "but
it should not be so to you." To this he quickly answered, "Yes; but
my shortcomings—my shortcomings!" How, he pondered, could he ever
approach a holy God when his own life had been so sinful, so imperfect? He had always recognized, quite properly, that man is not saved
by his own good works, but by the grace of God through faith in Christ.
Man needed to be born again to enter the Kingdom of God. Yet, his
defects weighed so heavily on his mind that he continually wondered
whether or not he had experienced true regeneration. Were not, he queried, his own imperfections a hint that he had never truly been born again?

Happily, Frelinghuysen did not die with such uncertainty on his heart. At some point during the closing weeks, his doubts disappeared. God gave him the peace which he so coveted. The resolution did not occur instantly, and many factors contributed to it: the support of his friends and colleagues, the love of his family, the testimony of Scripture. But one event did predominate. At the right moment, a friend placed before him a poem by the English writer (Mrs.) A.L. Waring. In these lines he found assurance:

> I love to think that God appoints
> My portion day by day;
> Events of life are in His hand,
> And I would only say,
> Appoint them in thine own good time,
> And in thine own best way.
>
> All things shall mingle for my good,
> I would not change them if I could,
> Nor alter Thy decree.
> Thou art above and I below,
> Thy will be done, and even so,
> For so it pleaseth Thee.

Frelinghuysen quoted these lines to another visitor a few days before his death, acknowledging the depth of comfort they afforded him. "The last weeks of his life I was constantly with him," said this same friend. "[Frelinghuysen] was [thereafter] always cheerful, sometimes indulging in pleasantry, in alluding to old anecdotes and scenes, and he never for a moment doubted his entire safety in the Redeemer."

Heart

I've mentioned Frelinghuysen's fear of death as a way of introducing a few comments about his personality and his spiritual development, especially about his "defects." They did exist; he was not a perfect Christian. He had character traits which limited his witness and undermined his effectiveness as a leader.

Surprisingly, neither his political opponents nor today's scholars are much help with documenting his personal defects. Both of these communities fault him primarily for his "Christian Whiggery," a philosophy either profoundly threatening or naive to them, depending on their own political or religious perspectives. About the only personal shortcoming—mentioned by Clifford S. Griffin—was Frelinghuysen's "extraordinary love of eating," though why this was particularly troublesome remains unclear.

His family and friends, however, despite their overwhelmingly positive portrait, suggested three types of interrelated shortcomings. First, there was a certain "harshness" in his mood, a curtness with others which some friends found unsettling. This occurred especially during times when he was physically ill. His nephew, Talbot Chambers, noted that trait several times when commenting about his beloved uncle. Second, Chambers also mentioned Frelinghuysen's more general irritability, what he called his uncle's "infirmities of temper and temperament." Reading between the lines, I judge this to be a reference to Frelinghuysen's tendency to criticize others when they did not strive for excellence or live up to their potential—a "natural" trait in light of his own concern for works as an expression of true faith. Third, several friends observed his difficulty in dealing with stressful situations, *per se*. He did not handle tension as well as he would have liked. During the final few years at New York University, for example, the strain brought about by the university's financial plight damaged his emotional and physical health. I have previously referred to this stage of "disordered nerves," using the phrase employed by several of his contemporaries. He was, in short, a worrier and one who on occasion could be quite critical of others.

A great fear of death and an inordinate sense of his own sinfulness, as noted in the introduction to this chapter, were the most debilitating features of his spiritual walk. They kept him from experiencing fully the Christian's sense of pervasive inner peace which perhaps would have made his Christian life even more effective. Perhaps. But I shouldn't dwell on the negative, for it was greatly outweighed by the positive, by Frelinghuysen's generally well-rounded personality and remarkable piety. It should be obvious from the previous chapters that Frelinghuysen had a heart for God and lived accordingly.

It would thus be much more accurate, when assessing his life, to accept the judgment of Dr. Woodbridge of the Dutch Reformed Seminary in New Brunswick: "I have many a time thought that, were a skeptic to ask for the living testimony of the power of the Gospel on the heart and life of man to make him true, and honest...I would point him to Theodore Frelinghuysen, and ask an explanation of such a life and death." Family and friends lavished praise on Frelinghuysen. They generally found him to be amiable, courteous, trustworthy, humble, humorous, a good listener as well as an apt weaver of tales, and a lover of children and family life.

His spiritual life too was of the highest caliber. Despite his shortcomings (one of which was not even public knowledge), he was a spiritual leader, a model of true spirituality to those around him. He was a man of prayer, beginning and ending each day on his knees before God. In addition, he spent fifteen minutes in prayer in the middle of each day. Bible reading and study were foundational to all his day's activities. A typical example of his dependence on both types of spiritual exercises occurred during his time in Washington, D.C. Upon arrival, he was appalled by the lack of spiritual health in the nation's capital. His remedy, begun in 1832, was the formation of a congressional prayer meeting and Bible study. Leaders, above all, should be on their knees and close to Scripture, he believed.

In the final analysis, Frelinghuysen's heart was always *searching* for God and God's will. At times, this prevented him from sensing that God had already *found* him and would freely give peace to the searching heart. Yet, he was still largely a positive, spiritual model for his contemporaries and remains so for us today. For we too need spiritual peace but not complacency. The following description of Frelinghuysen by his friend, Tayler Lewis, could thus represent us all:

> Mr. Frelinghuysen had difficulties in his religious life, in his personal experience, and he would freely tell them. His whole soul was in the pilgrimage to the New Jerusalem....[He] was still but a *"seeker of salvation."* This was ever the form of his thought and the spirit of his language....[He] regarded himself [and other Christians] as a company of earth-weary, heaven-seeking pilgrims, marching hand in hand...until at last the heavenly land is reached by all, the weakest as well as the strongest in the band.

Home

Frelinghuysen was committed to the Christian home. He believed it to be a "foundational" institution similar to the church as a basic building block for a Christian nation. It was in the home where children were taught the essentials of the Christian faith and where they learned how to live out their faith by observing their parents as role models. Building a Christian home was thus a heavy responsibility for parents, but one which they were to accept joyfully and optimistically; for God had given them the necessary equipment for construction: the Holy Spirit and the Word. Concerning the latter, he confessed to a friend in 1853: "The...blessings of the family relation can never be enjoyed, long or fully, without the hallowed influence of the Bible, in the purity and power of its principles and the supports of its unfailing consolations."

The Christian home was to be viewed as a partnership. For his partner, he chose Charlotte Mercer, daughter of a well-known businessman. One friend described her as "a lady of numerous graces of person and manner." She had a buoyant personality which helped her husband rebound from his occasional emotional setbacks. Charlotte and Theodore were inseparable companions for more than forty years, before death severed their union in 1854.

The death of his wife was a great shock to him. He probably could not have survived a loss of this magnitude without the support of family and friends. They surrounded him with love and encouraged him to continue with his professional duties. To them, Theodore remained the patriarch. In this loving context, therefore, the pain of Charlotte's death gradually healed. In 1857 he married Miss Harriet Pompelly, seeking and finding in her a substantial degree of the companionship he had enjoyed with his first wife. Harriet, a woman of "great intellectual and moral worth," was his greatest comfort in the last months of his declining health.

The Frelinghuysen home was famous for its hospitality. People came for dinner and stayed late into the night for stimulating conversation. People came to visit and stayed the whole night or for several days. All kinds of people passed through the "revolving door," agents of benevolent associations, ministers of any denomination, family members, friends and associates from faraway places, and especially students. The spiritual seekers also found an open door. One astonished woman, upon witnessing the parade of visitors being graciously welcomed, declared, "Mr. Frelinghuysen is making his house a house of refuge." Overhearing her remark, Theodore replied, "Such I would have it to be."

Why did Frelinghuysen become "Mr. Host" and his home a refuge to any and all visitors? The answer, I believe, is twofold. First, loving people, he hated being alone and coveted the fellowship of others. Second, he was compensating for a painful vacuum in his life, namely, the sad fact that the Frelinghuysens had no children of their own. Childlessness must have been a heavy burden to a man who loved children as much as he did. No doubt, the sound of visitors, especially visitors with small children, must have been a bittersweet presence in his home.

But being a host was not the only way to compensate for childlessness. Quite early in Theodore's married life adopting children became a possibility for him and Charlotte. The particular circumstances surrounding adoption for Frelinghuysen were tragic, but God was able to turn sadness into joy over time.

The Frelinghuysens adopted three children, a nephew and niece of his and a nephew of Charlotte's. Each adoption proceeding was initiated after the death of one or both of the natural parents. The first one was the saddest. In 1820, as you recall, Theodore's brother Frederick died. He left behind a three-year-old son, Frederick Theodore, his uncle's namesake. (It was apparent even in 1817 that Theodore's own marriage might be forever childless.) With the consent of Frederick's widow, Theodore's nephew came into his household as his adopted son.

No better example of Theodore's "family" leadership could be found than in his relationship with Frederick Theodore. Theodore lavished upon him all the love and discipline of a natural father. He taught him to cherish the Word, to pray without ceasing, and to make the church an important part of his life. And the so-called "secular" pursuits were not neglected either. "[Theodore] delighted in giving...his namesake every advantage in the ways of education and culture," declared one historian in 1925. Theodore sponsored his namesake's education from grammar school through Rutgers, then trained him at law in his own office from 1836 to 1839. In brief, every aspect of Frederick Theodore's education and life was guided by his stepfather. He was raised to be a Christian, and great things were expected of him. And great things he accomplished!

When his uncle accepted the chancellorship of New York University in 1839, Frederick Theodore took over his legal practice in Newark. He was an able successor, displaying his uncle's sharp legal mind and oratorical eloquence. For two decades he served as one of Newark's premier private attorneys, being retained by powerful clients such as the New Jersey Central Railroad and the Morris Canal and Banking Company. During some of these years, he also served as Newark's city attorney. His legal career crested in 1861 with his appointment as New Jersey's attorney general.

Frederick Theodore's legal fame led to a meteoric political career. At the conclusion of the Civil War, he was appointed to the U.S. Senate as a Republican, holding office until 1869. In 1871 he was again appointed senator and served out his full six-year term. In the Senate, his committee work was renowned, especially his chairmanship of the agriculture committee. Finally, in 1881, following the assassination of President Garfield, he was appointed by President Chester Arthur as secretary of state. From this exalted position, he negotiated several important treaties, though his favorite project—a treaty calling for the building of a canal through Nicaragua—was not ratified.

Theodore would have been just as proud of his adopted son's accomplishments in the "spiritual" realm. He continued, for example, to devote his energies in several leadership positions to the Dutch Reformed Church, the church of their ancestors. He was also a champion, like his uncle, of benevolent societies. Perhaps nothing would have warmed Theodore's heart more than the knowledge that his namesake would one day function as president of the American Bible Society.

Frederick Theodore was an excellent example of the truth of the Biblical challenge to "bring up a child in the way that he should go, and he will not depart from it."

Sanctuary

I suggested earlier that Frelinghuysen's life was unusual because much of his leadership was exercised outside of the boundaries of the institutional church. Yet, he did not ignore this important institution either, functioning, as well, as a church leader. Where he found the time is a mystery!

All of his church life—approximately forty-five years—was spent in the context of Presbyterian and Reformed denominations. As mentioned previously, his first adult church contact was in Newark where he helped form the Second Presbyterian Church in 1811. He participated as a leader there as a member of the board of trustees and as a Sunday School teacher. While in Newark as private attorney and as mayor, this church was the focus of a good share of his attention. It was there, remember, where he was received into full communicant membership in 1817.

The attraction of his ancestral or Dutch Reformed Church, however, proved irresistible, and he eventually transferred his membership and primary loyalty to this second type of Reformed communion. Why the shift? Talbot Chambers summarized it well:

> [Frelinghuysen] cherished a warm attachment for the ancestral Church....[This] was the result not only of hereditary associations...but also of a discriminating appreciation for her doctrine, and order, and discipline, and spirit. Hence, although he was first admitted to the Lord's table at a Presbyterian church, and continued long and happily in that connection, yet, as soon as Providence opened the way, he returned with alacrity, and joy to the Church of his fathers.

The first communion to benefit from the reunion was the famous Collegiate Church in New York City. He joined this church shortly after his arrival in the city to assume his duties as chancellor of New York University. It was from here that he was first elected by the Synod of the Dutch Reformed Church in 1846 as a member of the Board of Corporation, a synodical ruling body. He would subsequently fill this office every year except one until his death in 1862.

It was in this congenial environment that he also accepted the position of ruling elder. As elder, a friend reported, he particularly enjoyed regular visitation of the sick and elderly and "guarding the peace" of the church. Protecting the church's peace was crucial because he wanted the Dutch Reformed Church to avoid the tragic internal battles which had split the Presbyterian Church in 1837. He thus coveted the title of "peacemaker."

Accepting the presidency of Rutgers in 1850 also meant inauguration of the final chapter of his church life. Many citizens of New Brunswick no doubt expected him to select the First Reformed Church as his home. After all, First Church was the most prestigious sanctuary in town, one blessed by memberships of past college presidents and local elites. Yet, he chose to join the Second Reformed Church, just then being organized. Second Church had little prestige but many needs, a choice, I believe, that was fitting and typical of Frelinghuysen's style of leadership.

Two remaining features of his church ministry need to be noted. First, his leadership was not limited to regular church worship services or activities confined to the Sabbath: the whole week opened up to him avenues of service. Midweek prayer meeting especially received his support and guidance along with other times of Bible study and social activity. Second, his leadership was undertaken in close working relationship with his pastors, who respected his insight and relied on his devotion to the cause of worship and spiritual growth. Particularly cordial partnerships developed with Rev. Dr. Hay, his pastor from 1822 to 1833 and with Rev. Thomas DeWitt, his pastor at the Collegiate Church in New York City.

Frelinghuysen's commitment to Scripture has been amply documented. "You will find," he reiterated in 1831, "an unfailing fountain of hope in the promises of the Bible, of which neither sorrow nor death can deprive you." The Bible was to be the indispensable recipe book in the planning of life's activities:

> Let any member of society, in whatever supposable case of controversy with his neighbor, go honestly to the Bible for direction, and he will not be ignorant as to what is right and proper for him to do. Or let a citizen, who would learn the true measure of his duty to the commonwealth in a point beyond the reach of the statute-book, search the scriptures, and see if there not be a rule of unerring guidance there for him.

Following the Bible, in sum, would give America and Americans several blessings: national prosperity, liberty, charitable hearts, principled education, morality, personal salvation, and comfort in times of trouble.

But what of formal theology *per se?* What are the best labels for it; why, that is, have I been calling it "evangelical" and also "Reformed"? The task of labeling Frelinghuysen's theology is difficult because he did not speak the language of Biblical or systematic theology. He was theologically sophisticated but did not express the deep theological reflection characteristic of a theologian. He was simply a well-trained layman who lived his faith. Moreover, the distinction between "evangelical" and "Reformed" is more suited to our own age, an age when labels like these and "fundamentalist" have assumed shades of meaning unknown to our predecessors. Nonetheless, some distinctions can be made.

I consider his theology evangelical because (1) it was conservatively Christian in his submission to a general confession like the Apostles' Creed, (2) it stressed the "evangel," the gospel of salvation freely offered to all who would believe, (3) it was ecumenical in that it drew support from and recognized all (Protestant) denominations as allies in spreading the good news, and (4) it emphasized the "social implications" of the Christian faith.

But his theology was also Reformed because (1) it stressed themes like the Lordship of Christ and the Kingdom of God, (2) it acknowledged Christ's Lordship over all areas of life, that all spheres and realms be-

110

longed to Him, (3) it claimed that the "secular" spheres of especially politics and education must be redeemed by Christians, and (4) implicitly it acknowledged that by accepting one's calling and using one's gifts in areas like politics and education, spiritual service was being done. The gospel, thus, had more than social implications; it *was* political and educational in its message.

When I regard Frelinghuysen's life, I see an almost perfect blend of evangelicalism and the Reformed faith. He somehow preserved the best features of both while managing to avoid their pitfalls.

Death of a Saint

Theodore Frelinghuysen's last year on earth was a momentous one for America. The winds of war were blowing; in fact, the sounds of the first shots drifted north on April 12, 1861, exactly one year before his death. He was, on the one hand, of patriotic stock and found it easy to support President Lincoln's desire to preserve the Union. On May 23, 1861, at a special rally on Rutgers' campus, he gave one of his last public orations, promising New Jersey's governor that the Union army could count on many volunteers from the student body.

Yet, on the other hand, he was also a man of peace. He realized how horrible war could be and prayed earnestly for a cessation of hostilities. He was deeply saddened by the reports of carnage and brutality coming from the initial battles. He wanted to live long enough to see a quick end to the war and the preservation of the Union.

But this was not to be the case. The winter of 1861-62 brought him great physical distress. Early in the winter he caught a severe cold; it lingered, and his strength declined. As the winter unfolded, he experienced painful stomach problems, finding it difficult to eat certain foods and digest what he had consumed. Both he and those around him, as I have suggested, seemed to realize that death approached. When the end finally came in the following spring, he had reached the age of seventy-five. Although he was troubled by physical pain and distressed by the continuing Civil War, he had made his peace with God. His final words came in response to a question from his close friend, William Campbell. "Is it peace with you now?" "All peace," he whispered, "more than ever before."

The funeral service took place in the Reformed Church in New Brunswick on April 16, 1862. In all respects, the ceremonies were evidence of the esteem in which Frelinghuysen was held by both the Christian and secular communities. Mourners came, for example, not only from New Brunswick but also from throughout New Jersey as well as from New York State and Pennsylvania. Flags in New Brunswick were flown at half-mast, places of business were closed, and church bells tolled. Pallbearers included the governor and chief justice of New Jersey, the chancellor of Rutgers, and the president of Princeton University; twelve other distinguished citizens attended. Eulogies were given by Rev. J. Few Smith of Newark, Rev. Thomas DeWitt of the Collegiate Church, and Professor William Campbell, his friend and successor as president of Rutgers. Theodore Frelinghuysen was laid to rest in the cemetery adjoining the First Reformed Church, where so many other presidents and professors of Rutgers had been buried.

Following his death, tributes poured in from everywhere. The Synod of the Reformed Church lamented the "departure of a man of such high distinction and eminent worth, and who has so long served both his country and the Church in elevated positions of influence and responsibility." Newspaper editorials and obituaries, such as the *Sentinel of Freedom* (Newark) and the *Newark Daily Advertiser*, praised him for his "goodness," his "piety," and his leadership qualities exhibited as a lawyer, politician, and educator.

Perhaps the most fitting tribute came from one of his nephews, who claimed that the "fundamental element" in Frelinghuysen's life was "his simple and absolute faith in the Lord Jesus Christ as the Lamb of God that taketh away the sins of the world." This Christian leader, noted the same source, had never led a dualistic life, one where religion was reduced to a neat little spiritual compartment, carefully protected from secular concerns. Frelinghuysen's life was of a different sort:

> His religious faith interpenetrated his whole life, and gave to it its characteristic tone. He was just as much a Christian in the court-room, or on the floor of the Senate, or at the hustings, as in his closet, or the Sunday-school, or a prayer-meeting.

I can only add a hearty "Amen" to that description!

* * * * * * *

Discussion Questions

1. Is it ever appropriate for Christian leaders to express doubts about their faith? Why or why not? What of the "fear of death"? Do we expect too much from our leaders? In other words, do we expect them to be perfect?

2. How can we help leaders who are under enormous pressure? Name some ways.

3. Which of Frelinghuysen's positive personal traits do you find most attractive? Why?

4. Frelinghuysen's relationship with his two wives was very close. Is this what we expect from our leaders? To what extent can a man or

woman be a leader when the marriage is not very strong? Is it preferable for a leader to be a celibate?

5. Frelinghuysen turned his house into a "house of refuge." To what extent is this desirable or even possible for leaders today? or even for Christians who are not in leadership positions?

6. Frelinghuysen's marriage was childless and he turned to adoption. To what extent should we expect today's leaders to follow his example? Or does childlessness provide a greater opportunity for Christian service of other kinds?

7. What does Frelinghuysen's relationship with his nephew, Frederick Theodore, tell us about him and his leadership?

8. What does Frelinghuysen's choice of membership in the newly-formed Second Reformed Church of New Brunswick tell us about his leadership?

9. Frelinghuysen had a close and mutually supportive relationship with his various pastors. Is this what we expect from Christian leaders who minister to the "secular" realm?

10. I've called Frelinghuysen's theology a perfect blend of evangelicalism and the Reformed faith. Do you agree? Do we need to see more of this mixture from our leaders? What is missing from this particular synthesis?

11. I've suggested that for Frelinghuysen life was "religion." Would you agree?

12. To what extent do we need to see more leaders like Frelinghuysen? Name some things we can do to increase the likelihood of having more leaders such as he was.

Chapter 12

Leadership

> If provoked, [Daley will] break into a rambling, ranting speech, waving his arms, shaking his fists, defending his judgment, defending his administration, always with the familiar "It is easy to criticize...to find fault...but where are your programs...where are your ideas...?" Every word of criticism must be answered, every complaint must be disproved, every insult returned in kind. He doesn't take anything from anybody.
> —Mike Royko on Richard J. Daley, 1971

> During his residence in this city as Chancellor of the University of New York, [Frelinghuysen] frequently presided at the meetings of the Board of Managers, where his presence was ever welcomed and his counsels were valued. He adorned his place with peculiar dignity, grace...administrative ability...[and] courtesy.
> —William J. R. Taylor on Frelinghuysen, 1863

Before I review the various dimensions or characteristics of Christian leadership which I have discovered in my study of Frelinghuysen, I want to present three instances from my own personal experience where I judged leadership to be lacking. Each deals with politics, though similar stories could no doubt be recounted from all areas where Christians minister to the world.

I once interviewed a man who worked for a Christian politician holding office at the national level. During the course of the interview, I asked this man, also a Christian, to explain why the politician belonged to the Republican rather than the Democratic party. "Because he believes in Republican principles," came the immediate response. "What principles in particular?" I probed. He then rose and went to a file, rummaged through it for a minute, discovered what he was looking for, and placed the single page before me. "I believe this accurately summarizes the congressman's basic Republican principles," he beamed. I read with interest the list placed before me. Here is what "Republicanism" meant to these two leaders: a sound dollar, a strong defense, opposition to Soviet expansionism, religious liberty, and equal opportunities for all individuals to achieve financial security. By biting my inner lip, I managed to keep from laughing. After a moment, I asked this associate which of these "Republican" principles would be rejected by Democrats. He perused the list for a few seconds. He then began to look a little sheepish. "I see your point," he quietly confessed.

I had a similar opportunity fairly recently to pursue the question of party politics with another Christian politician. At the time we spoke, he was the head of a federal bureaucracy in Washington, D. C., after completing several terms in the House of Representatives. I introduced myself as a Christian and made it clear to him that I was pleased with the number of evangelicals in positions of prominence in the nation's capital. I also congratulated him on the degree of spiritual fellowship he and other Christians had developed. I then inquired about the depth of political fellowship which existed. "Well, political fellowship is a little more limited," he admitted. "We are still divided along party lines." "What about the Christians' commitment to the two-party system?" I queried. "I'm surprised you asked that question. We're *absolutely* committed to the two-party system." "What about alternatives to the two-party system?" I further probed. "Do any of you ever consider other options?" At this point, he became visibly annoyed. "We are all opposed to any type of one-party system," he proclaimed. "One-party systems are totalitarian and must be opposed at all costs by Christians! Again, I'm surprised that you asked this question." Well, I hadn't really asked about one-party systems, but his answer was certainly revealing!

My final example of today's (mis)leadership is even more pointed. A few years ago I had the chance to present highlights of my political philosophy to a Christian acquaintance who had political ambitions. At the time of this interaction, he had just finished an unsuccessful bid for national elective office. (He remained hopeful, though, of victory further down the road.) He listened courteously to my philosophy and responded with his own political theories. After a time, our conversation settled on more practical issues. "What do you think of gun control legislation?" he queried. I tried to explain my position of rather strict regulation, especially for handguns. He looked skeptical. I asked, "What is your approach to gun control? Forget for a moment rifles for sporting purposes. Concentrate on handguns." "I used to hold your perspective," he acknowledged. "But I changed my mind lately." He went on to explain why strict handgun regulations could be counterproductive. It boiled down to his perception that handguns were needed to protect us from criminals. I pointed out that most murders were committed by friends and relatives and that the presence of a gun could actually increase the chances of the owner being physically harmed. He countered with his "evidence," and we went back and forth, inconclusively.

I finally fell back on what I thought would be common ground: prohibition of "Saturday night specials," those cheap and poorly made weapons formerly so easy to obtain, at least in certain states. "Surely," I implored, "we must outlaw them?" But even here we parted company. "Even they might serve a useful purpose," he concluded. How, I inquired, could he defend these questionable weapons? His answer was simple. "They are needed by the poor, especially the urban poor. Poor people can't afford to spend $100 to $150 on a regular pistol, one you buy in a legitimate gun shop. They can only afford to purchase Saturday night specials. At least this provides some protection for them." The reply was disappointing and did not speak at all to the danger to the owner of just his possessing the gun.

These episodes present a pretty dark picture of the "conventional wisdom" prevalent among contemporary Christian leaders. If true of the community at large, they indicate that we are so tied to our culture, so ignorant of other traditions, so driven by every modern wind that we frequently have little to offer our fellow citizens. Why, for example, should the secular world be impressed when Christians don't realize that there is very little difference between our two major political parties; when, similarly, we fail to acknowledge that one alternative to our two-party system is not totalitarianism but the common practice of multiparty politics found throughout western Europe; and when we fall victim to such strange logic as I've just mentioned relative to gun control? We should be more aware of the complex moral and political implications involved in such problematic issues.

That is why I am so encouraged by the life of Theodore Frelinghuysen. Here was a man who, though fallible, rose above many of the commonplaces of his day. What follows is a summary of the characteristics of Christian leadership which I see Frelinghuysen embodying and some attempts to make these relevant to our contemporary situation as evangelicals and Reformed Christians. Read critically—accepting, rejecting, revising, adding. Reach out and make Frelinghuysen and the lessons from his life a part of your own.

1. Piety

A Christian leader needs to be truly pious, to have a dynamic living faith. Frelinghuysen was such a man. Prayer, Bible reading, and family devotions were foundational to his life. As a result, he led a life of evolving sanctification.

You might ask why I even bring up this point; don't we assume piety in our Christian leaders? Yes we do, but sometimes too readily, I think. Over the years, I have been impressed with how much we focus on announcements of one's "born-again" status and church attendance as signs of piety. But we can be mistaken. I don't just mean that some leaders pretend to be Christians for political purposes. I am referring to sincere Christian leaders who have lost their anchor, who no longer experience deeply the walk of faith and personal holiness. That is a very sad situation because we cannot expect to receive normative direction from those who are personally adrift on our secular sea. Those who have lost the ability to be like "little children" in their spiritual walk do not deserve many followers.

2. A Passion for Souls

I'm convinced that piety leads to a concern for the spiritual welfare of others. It certainly did for Frelinghuysen. Personal evangelism was one of the hallmarks of his life. He never let a chance slip away to speak to others for Christ.

But why is this a characteristic for leadership? The answer is simply because we are all called to speak for Christ when the opportunity arises. Yet, this imperative seems to be neglected by many leaders today, at least those outside the institutional church. I have interviewed and interacted with many political, educational, and business leaders in recent years and few seem to give high priority to evangelism. Evangelism is someone else's business; they have other jobs to perform. I can understand and accept this logic up to a point. But it can also be an excuse. And the results can be tragic. Perhaps some of our most famous and powerful leaders have never been reached personally by the call of the gospel.

I realize the courage such speaking out takes. It's a lot easier to talk to Senator_____ about the Salt II Treaty or farm subsidies than about his need of a Savior. Who knows how he'll respond. Who knows . . .

Henry Clay was not too "big" to be touched by the missionary hand of Theodore Frelinghuysen. Are there Frelinghuysens around today in politics and elsewhere who care enough about the eternal questions to begin reaching out to their peers more purposefully? I hope so. I also hope that in reviewing the life of Frelinghuysen they will be stimulated to greater efforts.

3. A Strong Self-Image

A Christian leader needs to be confident of his talents and aware of his limitations. In other words, he needs to have a strong self-image. Frelinghuysen had such inner strength. He did not withdraw from public life after losing his Senate seat in 1835 nor abandon education after fighting New York University's financial crisis for many years. He did not despair when losing the race for the vice-presidency in 1844. He realized that God had given him the talents and inner resources to be an effective leader. He simply had to exercise them.

But at the same time Frelinghuysen also recognized the importance of Christian community. He did not try to save the world all by himself; his own sins and deficiencies were all too painfully obvious to him. Only the Body of Christ had the power to advance the Kingdom toward its consummation.

Many Christian leaders today seem to have lost this precarious and precious balance. Some seem obsessed with their own power and importance. One such sad specimen told a friend of mine that he would not allow anything to interfere with his work or the growth of his organization. Others are easily discouraged, quick to abandon a ministry or calling when troubles erupt. Christians holding political office are some of the most vulnerable to this kind of despair. Politics can be extremely frustrating to those who enter her sanctuary with naivete. They, above all, need the inner strength that Frelinghuysen recognized as coming from a supportive Christian community.

4. A Sense of History

No leader can make a substantial normative contribution to a sphere or an issue without a sense of history. This is especially true of Christians. We are both a people of the "Book" and people rooted in an historical religion. No better example of such a truth could be found than Frelinghuysen. His feet were firmly planted in "redemptive history," the story of salvation in Christ. And he loved American history, the saga of a free people. Thus he strongly supported the study of American history and European history, fields laden with the seeds of liberty. One of his favorite causes, for example, was that of historical societies. "The Uses and Benefits of Historical Societies," an 1852 speech of his before the New Jersey Historical Society, gives us a concise summary of his rationale for the study of history.

Too many leaders today seem to lack both a sense of history and an awareness of the lessons of history. Consequently, they are cut off from their roots, floating around, ignorant of their past, uncertain of their future—or "certain" of it, yet making the same mistakes as their predecessors. A good example of what this ignorance produces was revealed recently in my presence. I was discussing the lessons to be learned from American political history with a Christian leader when suddenly he became very excited. "The basic solution to our political problems is ethical leadership," he proclaimed. "We need ethical leaders, leaders who cannot be bribed and who will be morally clean." By ethical, of course, he meant Christian. After he calmed down a bit, I reminded him that Christians are not necessarily more moral than many humanists and that such a concentration on personal ethics obscured any of the

119

systematic ills of American politics. How often we all seem to return to the ''let's throw out the rascals'' theme. We rarely focus on the need of the system for reformation. I'm not sure that this particular histori- cal lesson of the need for the system's reformation would have occurred as forcefully to Frelinghuysen. But it occurs to me.

5. A Concern for Youth

The future must also be important to leadership, not just the future as a general theme but the future of our covenant youth, both the lead- ers and the followers of the next and subsequent generations. Freling- huysen pressed this truth close to his heart. He loved the company of children and considered educational ministry to young people as one of life's highest callings.

The importance of youth is a theme proclaimed by many. Yet some leaders seem to give mere lip service to the nurturing of tomorrow's Frelinghuysens, not following through with a willing effort to lead young potential leaders into the educational experiences they need. Two rea- sons for this appalling oversight stand out in my mind. First, the sin of present*ism* is a factor. I know of leaders who get so caught up in their own crusades and causes that the next generation is pushed aside, or at least is required to submit to a ''delayed adolescence,'' patiently waiting in the wings until this generation of leaders finally realizes it must step aside. Second, a certain kind of dispensational pre- millennialism can be a cause. I know of one Christian leader, for ex- ample, who sees little reason to prepare carefully the leaders of tomor- row because there will be no tomorrow! Not all dispensationalists hold a similar view, by any means, but it is a factor to be considered in light of the rapid development of this phenomenon within evangelical circles.

Other leaders go to the opposite extreme, fostering a kind of self- serving hero-worship on the part of their disciples. They can visualize *nothing* as crucial as training tomorrow's leadership. They talk about this glorious task all the time and surround themselves with adoring young people who tape all their lectures and devour all their articles and books. I'm not sure which is more depressing—insecure ''leaders'' who require so many emotional strokes or thoughtless disciples who confuse submission with growth. At any rate, normative unfolding is unlikely in such a warped environment.

6. An Effective Communicator

Effective communication is a prerequisite to good leadership. A leader who is deficient in communication skills is almost a contradiction in terms. Such a deficiency, as you recall, was not Frelinghuysen's problem; he was a communicator par excellence. ''Spellbinding'' and ''gripping'' were typical labels used to describe his oratory and rhetoric. He knew how to turn a phrase and present an argument. Of all his gifts, perhaps this ability to communicate publicly was the greatest.

Today we live in a world where communication is no less important, yet where oratory has become virtually a lost art (or an underused gift). The oration has been replaced by the harangue, persuasion by propaganda; the medium has become the message. The potential for abuse has thus increased many fold.

How, then, can Christian leaders "communicate" normatively with an audience? How can we ensure that the medium does not become the message, at least the central message? These are crucial questions for our "electronic age," questions which our own "electronic church" is compelling us to ask.

I would argue that we have gone too far in accepting the world's communication agenda and approach. How can we claim effective communication by creating news programs based on thirty-second snippets, by interviewing *ad nauseum* Christian rock stars, and by broadcasting editorials which lambast our opponents, both "sacred" as well as secular? We need to put an end to such practices. Studying the life of a man like Frelinghuysen should give us a firm brake against this kind of accelerated foolishness. He knew both the content of his subject and the appropriate style in which it should be delivered. I cannot imagine a reincarnated Frelinghuysen pleading repeatedly for money over the airwaves or making an altar call by means of a taped sermon. He had too much respect for his audience and for his God.

7. A Holistic Perspective

Leaders need to project a unified vision of reality to their followers. God's people must hear that life is a beautiful, mysterious whole which cannot be easily broken up into antagonistic or unrelated compartments. Frelinghuysen, thankfully, was one of the first American Christians to advance this vision. In fact, he was so far ahead of his time that his rejection of "dualisms" sounds surprisingly modern. He would no doubt feel very much at home with our contemporary discussions about radical Christianity and Kingdom living.

The sacred-secular dualism was one of his favorite enemies. Consistent Christian living was made difficult, he believed, where this dichotomy existed. Though always stressing the importance of worship and the gospel, he moved close to our present confession, "All of life is sacred."

His ecclesiology was also progressive. He seemed to grasp intuitively the proper distinction between Church and church. The former refers to the Body of Christ, the latter to its institutional manifestation. Individual members of the Body of Christ, he argued, had to be involved actively in the world, fighting God's causes wherever they were led. But this did not automatically imply that the warfare was exclusively to be waged by the institutional church. Since the whole "secular" world also belonged to God, many other legitimate avenues of service existed and were usually preferable. What "liberation" this holistic perspective gave to Frelinghuysen and would give to us if we allowed it to gain an even stronger foothold!

8. A Multifaceted Service

The antebellum world could hardly provide us with a better example of Christian activism than Theodore Frelinghuysen— Emperor of the benevolent empire. Freed by his perspective from the narrow confines of *churchism*, he joyfully served God in a wide range of Christian institutions and causes. The institutional church received his attention too, but nonchurch, parachurch, and "secular" organizations and arenas benefited more from his gifts and talents. He was, in brief, the kind of layman that the Christian world so urgently needs today.

I still find, looking at today's emerging leadership, a tendency to focus energy upon the institutional church. What we need are more Rev. Springs to confront us with moral imperatives like "God requires laborers in state as well as church." Frelinghuysen could not deny this truth; nor, I pray, would many of today's future leaders—if it were forcefully, lovingly, and logically presented. Similar imperatives would force us to consider the life of Christian service as one which is as broad as the Kingdom itself. Primarily our talents and interests should limit our activities, not a narrow theology which exclusively exalts the institutional church.

But wouldn't this undermine the role of the church? Wouldn't a concentration of emerging leadership on nonchurch or "worldly" concerns make the church's task even more difficult? Again, the answer is "no." In fact, Frelinghuysen is proof that the opposite would occur, namely, a revitalization of the church. The reason should be obvious. If we follow Frelinghuysen's example and use our talents everywhere in God's creation, then the worshiping community becomes even more important. We recognize even more acutely our complete dependence upon God and our urgent need to praise Him and call upon Him to strengthen our life of service. Thus the worshiping-sacramental-confessional dimension of life truly assumes its proper, *central* place when we become activists like Frelinghuysen. The lesson is simple: a life of Christian activism *creates* meaningful worship!

Another blessing occurs when we follow Frelinghuysen's example. The church comes to realize that it doesn't have to save the world all by itself. Many other agencies and avenues exist to bring glory to God and healing to His creation. Once reminded of this truth, the church can concentrate on what it does best. She can then do it even better.

9. Courage

Courage is obviously a prerequisite to leadership, the courage to stand for principle or conscience, regardless of the consequences. Frelinghuysen's courageous stands have been amply documented: recall his Senate career and how it ended when he said "no" to Jackson and the New Jersey legislature on the issue involving the Bank of the United States and when he defended the orthodox Quakers against the Hicksites. Remember his defense of the black man charged with murder and his unpopular befriending of the Cherokees against the expansionism of the state of Georgia.

Happily, some examples exist in contemporary America of the courage of Christians in public life. Rev. Martin Luther King displayed such courage in his stand for racial justice in the 1950's and 1960's as did Senator Mark Hatfield in his challenge to two presidents to end the Vietnam war in the late 1960's and early 1970's. Others could be mentioned. I'm inclined, though, to believe that these are exceptions to the rule. Christian leaders, sadly, are not known for their courageous stands, apart from an obvious arena like abortion.

Why the paucity of principled stands? Perhaps some leaders have a difficult time establishing which principles are worth fighting for. Perhaps others can't formulate effective principles in the first place. Perhaps the majority simply don't want to "rock the boat," believing cautious incrementalism is the best policy. Maybe the answer is "all of the above and more." If so, the logic is self-evident: confused, anxious, even fearful "leaders" by definition won't take courageous stands. Whatever the reasons, our age doesn't seem to be producing very many Frelinghuysens.

10. A Christian Patriotism

Frelinghuysen's love of America is understandable. With his family heritage, something other than patriotism would be hard to imagine. His devotion, however, was tempered by Biblical insight, experience, and intuition, to the point where a normative "Christian patriotism" had begun to emerge.

In the turbulent 1980's, our own need for a similar normative patriotism is acute. President Reagan, a confessing Christian, is zealously leading Americans down the path of renewed nationalism. "The United States," we are told, "is the world's greatest nation, the last hope for preserving religious freedom and democracy in the world." I doubt whether Frelinghuysen would have made such a statement in his age, nor should we in ours. Neither the church nor "democracy" ultimately depends upon the strength of America but on the creative and redemp-

123

tive power of God through Christ. The proposition "God needs America" is true only inversely.

Swimming against the current of super-patriotism is not easy, yet this is what today's Christian leaders are called to do. If successful, we Christians will experience the shalom of a reality where love of America is "balanced" by respect for other members of the family of nations and "relativized" by a transcendent faith. And shalom is the business of leadership.

11. A Positive Government

The American System of Henry Clay provided Frelinghuysen with a basis for a vision of government which was a positive one. He therefore maintained, in contrast to the Jacksonians, that the state had an active role to play in the affairs of man. It could and must act, not only to preserve the peace, but to help stimulate the economy. It also had responsibility to bind up some of the wounds inflicted by the emerging industrial order.

Frelinghuysen's view of government as just described placed him in the vanguard of political thinking in his age. Unfortunately, it would also mark him as a progressive in the context of much of contemporary evangelical and Reformed thinking, for our own tradition during the last century was much more Jacksonian than "Frelinghuysenian." This situation should be reversed, not to encourage socialism, nor merely as a knee-jerk reaction against modern religious liberalism, but because Christianity *assumes* a positively active state. The institution of government is called by God to pursue a purposeful goal—justice—just as families, churches, colleges, and other institutions have necessary duties to perform. The proper stance for "conservative" Christians isn't to cry, "Get the state off our back," but to ask, "What is the nature of the problem before us?" and "What is the task of the government in resolving that problem?" The problem may require a big action by government or a small one, but a *response* is called for nonetheless. The state, no less than other institutions, groups, and individuals, has many valuable contributions to make to a healthy society. Christian leaders who inform us otherwise are making a serious mistake and would do well to pause and reflect upon the life of Theodore Frelinghuysen.

12. A Respected Leader

All of the traits mentioned so far have dealt with Frelinghuysen from an internal perspective, i.e., from the inside-looking-out. But what of the external perspective: what did others think of him? The answer is encouraging: he was almost universally respected as a leader, even by his political enemies. Hicksite attacks in 1834 and Democratic allega-

124

tions in 1844 were exceptions to the rule; normally, his stands won him high praise. His style being neither mean nor divisive, avoiding *ad hominem* arguments, Frelinghuysen traveled the high road of principle and conscience.

Today's Christian leaders would do well to emulate Frelinghuysen in this final area, too. It is natural for leaders to be loved by their immediate followers, but to be respected by one's enemies is another matter. What a powerful testimony, though, to the power of the gospel to bridge differences among adversaries.

The Road Less Traveled

How do we get there from here? How do we move in such a way as to increase the potential for seeing more leaders like Frelinghuysen appear on the horizon? Let me suggest the following course of action.

First, we need to pray for leaders, not just for existing leaders but for the appearance of new leaders. And our prayers should be specific. We should pray specifically that God would send us a Frelinghuysen, a William Jennings Bryan, a Martin Luther King, a Barbara Jordan, Christian leaders with definite characteristics which are needed in particular circumstances. Why should God send us the right kind of leader when we aren't making the appropriate request?

Second, the Bible must play an important role. We have to develop newer and better ways to read and interpret the Bible which allow us to understand its message about leadership more fully. Although not the center of the Biblical drama, statesmanship and leadership are vital subthemes appearing throughout Scripture—sometimes easily detected, at other times lying just beneath the surface. Much can be learned if we can somehow avoid the pitfalls of moralism. An additional prayer request, therefore, should be for God to open our eyes to greater truths from Scripture pertaining to leadership. Wouldn't He be more inclined to provide such help if we *specifically* ask for it?

Third, we can actively support leaders who have some of the traits of a Frelinghuysen. This is going to require a little work on our part, investigating, reaching out, questioning. The effort is necessary, however, because not everyone calling himself a leader is worthy of the name. Charlatans exist in the Christian community, and the sooner we face the fact the better off we'll be. On the other hand, there may also be potential Frelinghuysens out there who either aren't yet aware of their possibilities or feel isolated, unsupported, and must therefore be discovered, drawn out, and encouraged by a solid Christian community.

It is imperative in today's world to support leaders who are not wholly caught up in particular causes, crusades, or institutions. Politically, this means we shouldn't support Christians who are completely devoted to the cause of either major party. We don't need "Republican" Christians or "Democratic" Christians but individual Christians who *work within* each party for the cause of justice. Further, it would be encouraging and helpful to see leaders occasionally transcending conventional party labels by forming "third party" alternatives. Why are we so committed to the existing party framework? Frelinghuysen's commitment evolved from the Federalist party to the National-Republicans, on to the Whigs and finally stopping with the Republicans. Perhaps we should also consider an evolution of party loyalties and support leaders from any party who have the courage to create new options.

Fourth, through prayer, insight, experience, and hard work, some of *you* can *become* leaders. Do you have some leadership gifts? Then put them to the test in concrete situations, beginning with small tasks and seeing what God does with your faithful service. If you're a student, try the student council; if your interest is social concern, then volunteer to help with a Christian social work agency; if you're inclined toward politics, then do grassroots work for one of the existing parties—or better yet, help start a new one! There are plenty of ways to serve in God's world. He only waits for you to take the first step.

A Final Word

I began by saying that Chicago has suffered from a failure of leadership. In general, I would draw a similar conclusion about most American cities and for the nation as a whole. Reversing such a bleak trend will not be easy, but it must be done. And Christians are called to be in the forefront of the battle to discover new styles of leadership and to support those who show such signs of a "new creation." History doesn't provide us with all the answers. It is rewarding, nonetheless, when historical investigation rediscovers a man who has almost disappeared from our national consciousness and who then becomes a "fresh study," a model and inspiration for Christians who see the whole world, all of creation, as their field and responsibility. Perhaps the near future will bring us even more extensive work on the life of this particular Christian statesman.

A Select Bibliography

A. Primary Sources

1. Newspapers and Correspondence

The New Jersey State Historical Society in Newark and Rutgers University in New Brunswick house many of the relevant documents, though each collection is small. Both have some letters and documents relating to Frelinghuysen's personal life, legal career, and public life as a politician and educator.

The best newspapers for general background are: *Newark Daily Advertiser* (1832f), *Newark Morning Eagle* (1847-1853), *New Jersey Eagle* (Newark, 1847-1857), *Princeton Whig* (1834-1854), and *Sentinel of Freedom* (Newark, 1796-1862).

2. Book(s) by Theodore Frelinghuysen

Frelinghuysen's only book, published anonymously, was *An Inquiry into the Moral and Religious Character of the American People*. New York: Wiley & Putnam, 1838. It is a particularly rich source for political philosophy, especially questions relating to church and state and the possibility of a "Christian" America.

3. Articles, Speeches, and Addresses by Frelinghuysen (chronological):

"An Address Delivered Before the Newark Bible Society; on the Last Sabbath in June 1818, Being its Fourth Anniversary Meeting; in the Second Presbyterian Church in Newark." Newark: John Tuttle & Co., 1818. 11 p.

'The Constitution and Seventh Annual Report of the Female Auxiliary Bible Society of Newark, New Jersey, with an Address Delivered Before the Society, by Theodore Frelinghuysen, Esq., July 21, 1823." Newark, New Jersey: John Tuttle & Co., 1823. 6 p.

"An Oration: Delivered at Princeton, New Jersey, Nov. 16, 1824, Before the New Jersey Colonization Society, by the Honourable Theodore Frelinghuysen." Princeton Press, 1824. 10 p.

"An Address, Delivered in the Orange Church on the Evening of the 18th of December, 1826, Before the Members of the Society for the Education of Poor and Indigent Children of the Parish of Orange." Newark, New Jersey: W. Tuttle & Co., 1827. 8 p.

"Speech of Mr. Theodore Frelinghuysen of New Jersey, Delivered in the Senate of the United States, April 6, 1830, on the Bill for an Exchange of Lands with the Indians Residing in any of the States or Territories, and for their Removal West of the Mississippi." Washington: Office of the National Journal, 1836. 44 p.

"Speech of Mr. Frelinghuysen on His Resolution Concerning Sabbath Mails, Senate of the United States, May 8, 1830." Washington: Rothwell & Ustick, 1830. 12 p.

"An Address Delivered Before the Philoclean and Peithessophian Societies, Rutgers College." New Brunswick, New Jersey: Van Doorn and M'Cready, 1831. 19 p.

"Speeches of Messrs. Webster, Frelinghuysen and Others at the Sunday School Meeting in the City of Washington, Feb. 16, 1831." Philadelphia: American Sunday School Union, 1831. 10 p.

"Full Report of the Case of Stacy Decow, and Joseph Hendrickson, vs. Thomas L. Shotwell at the Special Term of the New Jersey Court of Appeals...July and August, 1833." Philadelphia: P.J. Gray, 1834. 94p.

"Speech of Mr. Frelinghuysen, on the Removal of the Deposites; Delivered in the Senate of the United States, January, 1834." Washington: Gales and Seaton, 1834. 15 p.

"Introduction," to Eddy, A.D. *The Duties, Dangers, and Securities of Youth.* New York: Leavitt, Lord, and Co., 1836, iiif.

"Statement on Temperance," *Trenton Reporter*, March 18, 1837, 20-22.

"Address Before the Merchants' Temperance Society in the City of New York, January 1842." New York: Office of the American Temperance Union, 1842. 6 p.

"Addresses etc. at the Inauguration of the Hon. Theodore Frelinghuysen as President of Rutgers College in New Brunswick at the Annual Commencement, July 1850." New Brunswick, New Jersey: J. Terhune Press, 1850. 9 p.

"The Uses and Benefits of Historical Societies, a Paper read before the New Jersey Historical Society, May 20, 1852." *Proceedings of the New Jersey Historical Society*, Vol. 6. 8 p.

"Henry Clay," (Eulogy), *New York Times*, July 15, 1852, 3.

"Introduction," to Cumming, John. *Is Christianity from God?* New York: M.W. Dodd, 1854, iii-v.

"Rutgers Commencement Address," *New York Times*, July 25, 1855, 1.

B. Biographies

Excellent as a primary as well as secondary source is Chambers, Talbot W. *Memoir of the Life and Character of the Late Hon. Theo. Frelinghuysen, LL.D.* New York: Harper and Brothers, 1863. Chambers was

Frelinghuysen's nephew by marriage. His study is understandably very positive. It is rich in anecdotes and in primary sources like letters to and from his uncle.

C. Secondary Sources

1. General Background Studies
   a. On Frelinghuysen: Helpful is a campaign biography by Parker, Cortlandt. *A Sketch of the Life and Public Services of Theodore Frelinghuysen.* New York: Tribune Office, 1844. Parker's focus is on Frelinghuysen's support of Henry Clay. Also see Folsom, Joseph ed. *The Municipalities of Essex County New Jersey.* New York: Lewis Historical Pub. Co., 1925. Vol. III; and Nothdurft, Ivan H. "Theodore Frelinghuysen," Manuscript of American Bible Society, New York, 1980. 15 p.
   b. On Antebellum America: For the premier study on religious history see Ahlstrom, Sidney E. *A Religious History of the American People.* New Haven, Conn.: Yale Univ. Press, 1972. Other good surveys of religious history and denominational history include Hudson, Winthrop S. *Religion in America.* New York: Charles Scribner's Sons, 1965; Olmstead, Clifton E. *History of Religion in the United States.* Englewood Cliffs, New Jersey: Prentice-Hall, Inc., 1960; Van Hoeven, James W. ed. *Piety and Patriotism: Bicentennial Studies of the Reformed Church in America,* 1776-1976. Grand Rapids, Mich.: Eerdmans Pub. Co., 1976; and DeJong, Gerald F. *The Dutch Reformed Church in the American Colonies.* Grand Rapids, Mich.: Eerdmans Pub. Co., 1978.

For classic studies on Jacksonian America see Schlesinger, Arthur M., Jr. *The Age of Jackson.* Boston: Little, Brown & Co., 1945; Myers, Marvin. *The Jacksonian Persuasion.* New York: Vintage Books, 1960; and Van Deusen, Glydon G. *The Jacksonian Era, 1828-1848.* New York: Harper and Brothers, 1959.

Two excellent studies of non-Reformed religious history by evangelicals are Smith, Timothy. *Revivalism and Social Reform in Mid-Nineteenth Century America.* Nashville, Tenn.: Abingdon, 1957; and Dayton, Donald W. *Discovering an Evangelical Heritage.* New York: Harper & Row, 1976.

2. Robert Finley and Richard Stockton
For studies of Finley, Frelinghuysen's mentor, see Brown, Isaac V. *Biography of the Rev. Robert Finley, D.D.* 2nd ed., enlarged. Philadelphia: John W. Moore, 1857; and Coulter, Merton E. *College Life in the Old South.* New York: The MacMillan Co., 1928. For the life and perspective of Federalist lawyer-politician Richard Stockton see Stockton, Thomas Coates. *The Stockton Family of New Jersey and Other Stocktons.* Washington: The Carnahan Press, 1911.

3. Antebellum New Jersey Politics

New Jersey politics is ably covered in Ershkowitz, Herbert. *The Origin of the Whig and Democratic Parties: New Jersey Politics, 1820-1837.* Washington: Univ. Press of America, 1982 (especially good on Frelinghuysen's early political struggles); Fee, Walter R. *The Transition from Aristocracy to Democracy in New Jersey, 1789-1829.* Somerville, New Jersey: Somerset Press, 1933; and McCormick, Richard P. "Party Formation in New Jersey in the Jacksonian Era," *Proceedings of the New Jersey Historical Society,* 83 (1965), 161-73. Also see McCormick, Richard P. *The Second American Party System: Party Formation in the Jacksonian Era.* New York: W.W. Norton, 1966.

4. Frelinghuysen's legal and political career

The best sources are the previously mentioned Chambers' *Memoir of the Life and Character of the Late Hon. Theo. Frelinghuysen;* Parker's *A Sketch of the Life and Public Services of Theodore Frelinghuysen;* and Folsom's *The Municipalities of Essex County New Jersey.* For Frelinghuysen's tenure as mayor see Morris, William W. *Biographical Sketches of Newark Mayors (1836-1905).* Newark: New Jersey Historical Society manuscript, n.d. 11 p. The background to what would soon become Frelinghuysen's "Quaker" problem is documented in Doherty, Robert. *The Hicksite Separation.* New Brunswick, New Jersey: Rutgers Univ. Press, 1967.

5. Henry Clay and the 1844 Presidential Election

Henry Clay's life is superbly covered in the following biographies: Schurz, Carl. *Henry Clay.* Boston and New York: Houghton Mifflin Co., 1887; Eaton, Clement. *Henry Clay and the Art of American Politics.* Boston: Little, Brown and Co., 1957; and Van Deusen, Glydon G. *The Life of Henry Clay.* Westport, Conn.: Greenwood Press, 1979. General studies which contain useful information on the 1844 election are Roseboom, Eugene H. *A History of Presidential Elections.* New York: The MacMillan Co., 1957; Nichols, Roy F. *The Invention of American Political Parties.* New York: The MacMillan Co., 1967; and Binkley, Wilfred E. *American Political Parties: Their Natural History,* 4th ed. New York: Alfred A. Knopf, 1962.

The authoritative study on Frelinghuysen's vice-presidential nomination is Hunt, William S. "Theodore Frelinghuysen: A Discussion of His Vice Presidential Candidacy in the Clay-Polk Campaign in 1844, and It's Reason's," *Proceedings of the New Jersey Historical Society,* 56 (1938), 30-40. Also of interest relating to the 1844 campaign are Graham, F.B. *Clay and Frelinghuysen Almanac, 1845.* New York: Turner and Fisher, 1844; and _____ . *Clay and Frelinghuysen Songster.* New York and Philadelphia: Turner and Fisher, n.d.

6. Whigs and Whiggery

The place to begin reading on the Whiggery in America is Howe, Daniel Walker. *The Political Culture of the American Whigs*. Chicago: Univ. of Chicago Press, 1979. Also see Poage, George Rawlings. *Henry Clay and the Whigs*. Gloucester, Mass.: Peter Smith, 1965; and the most recent study by Brown, Thomas. *Politics and Statesmanship: Essays on the American Whig Party*. New York: Columbia Univ. Press, 1985.

7. Colonization - Abolitionism

For the American Colonization Society and Frelinghuysen's contribution see the definitive study by Staudenraus, P.J. *The African Colonization Movement, 1816-1865*. New York: Columbia Univ. Press, 1961. For nineteenth century defenses also see Alexander Archibald. *A History of Colonization on the West Coast of Africa*. Philadelphia: William S. Martien, 1846; and _____. *Memorial of the Semi-Centennial Anniversary of the American Colonization Society*. Washington: Colonization Society Building 1867.

For the evangelical opposition to slavery see Wyatt-Brown, Bertram. *Lewis Tappan and the Evangelical War Against Slavery*. Cleveland: The Press of Case Western Reserve Univ., 1969. William Lloyd Garrison's shift from colonization to abolitionism is documented in the anthology by Thomas, John L. ed. *Slavery Attacked: The Abolitionist Crusade*. Englewood Cliffs, New Jersey: Prentice-Hall, Inc., 1965.

8. The Benevolent Empire

Benevolent associations are given critical treatments in the four books mentioned in this study: Griffin, Clifford S. *Their Brothers' Keepers, Moral Stewardship in the United States, 1800-1865*. New Brunswick, New Jersey: Rutgers Univ. Press, 1960; Cole, Charles C., Jr. *The Social Ideas of the Northern Evangelists, 1862-1860*. New York: Columbia Univ. Press, 1954; Bodo, John R. *The Protestant Clergy and Public Issues, 1812-1848*. Princeton, New Jersey: Princeton Univ. Press, 1954; and Foster, Charles I. *An Errand of Mercy: the Evangelical United Front, 1790-1837*. Chapel Hill, North Caro.: Univ. of North Carolina Press, 1960. Another classic negative treatment is Billington, Ray Allen. *The Protestant Crusade, 1800-1860*. Chicago: Quadrangle Books, 1964. For other general studies see Tyler, Alice Felt. *Freedom's Ferment*. New York: Harper & Row, 1944; and a recent investigation by Boyer, Paul. *Urban Masses and Moral Order in America, 1820-1920*. Cambridge, Mass.: Harvard Univ. Press, 1978.

Revisionist, more positive treatments are found in Banner, Lois W. "Religious Benevolence as Social Control: A Critique of an Interpretation," in Mulder, John M. and Wilson, John F. eds. *Religion in American History*. Englewood Cliffs, New Jersey: Prentice-Hall, Inc., 1978; and Matthews, Donald G. "The Second Great Awakening as an Organizing Process, 1780-1830: An Hypothesis,'' *American Quarterly*, 21 (Spring, 1969), 23-43.

For specific studies, which also refer to Frelinghuysen, see Strong, William E. *The Story of the American Board.* Boston: The Pilgrim Press, 1910, chapter VIII; Krout, John Allen. *The Origins of Prohibition.* New York: Alfred A. Knopf, 1925; and Garrison, William Lloyd. *Sonnets and Other Poems.* Boston: Oliver Johnson, 1843, 69-71.

9. Education

For Frelinghuysen's tenure at New York University see Chamberlain, Joshua L. ed. *New York University: Its History, Influence, Equipment and Characteristics.* Boston: Herndon Co., 1901. The years at Rutgers are covered in Demarest, William H.S. *A History of Rutgers College, 1766-1924.* New Brunswick, New Jersey: Rutgers College, 1924.

Index

A

Abolitionism, 61, 64f, 67-68
Adams, John Quincy, 11-12
Adams, Nehemiah, 76
Ahlstrom, Sidney, 71
American Bible Society, 43, 75f, 94, 108
American Board of Commissioners for Foreign Missions, 71, 73f
American Colonization Society, 60, 62, 67
American Sunday School Union, 77f
American System, 17-18, 41, 98
American Temperance Society, 78
American Temperance Union, 78f
American Tract Society, 43, 76f
An Inquiry into the Moral and Religious Character of the American Government, chapter 6 passim
Arthur, Chester, President, 108
Articles of Confederation, 23
Attorney General of New Jersey (Frelinghuysen), 10f, 60

B

Bank of United States (Second), 15-16, 24f, 29, 87
Banner, Lois, 72
Bateman, Ephraim, 11
Beck, Lewis C., 85
Beecher, Lyman, 54
Benevolent Empire, 48, 54, 62, chapter 8 passim
Benton, Thomas Hart, xiii, 21
Biddle, Nicholas, 26
Bodo, John, 49, 72
Bogard, John, 85
Bryan, William Jennings, x, 125
Burges, Tristram, 34

C

Calhoun, John, xiii
Campbell, William, 1, 4, 85, 93, 111-112
Cannon, James S., 85
Carter, Jimmy, x
Cass, Lewis, 79
Chamberlain, Joshua, 83-84
Chambers, Ezekiel F., 97, 101
Chambers, Talbot, 11, 15, 20, 30, 79, 82, 93-94, 96, 105, 109
Chancellor of New York University (Frelinghuysen), 40, chapter
  9 passim, 108-109, 115
Cherokee Indians, xiii, 20f, 27, 123
Christian confessionalism, 18f
Civil War (American), 62, 75, 79, 85, 108, 111
Clay, Henry, x, xiv, 15, 17-18, 29-30, 37-38, 41f, 45
  54, 59, 61, 78, 93, 98f, 118
Cole, Charles, 72
College of New Jersey (Princeton), 3, 8
Collegiate Church, New York City, 109-110, 112
Colonization, chapter 7 passim
Compassionate statism, 16f
Congressional Temperance Society, 79
Cook, George H., 85
Crosby, Howard, 81-82, 89-90, 95

D

Daley, Richard (Boss), ix, 115
Dallas, George, 37
Davis, John, 41
Davison, James, 24
Dayton, Donald, xv
Demarest, William, xiii, 61, 85
Democratic party, 15f, 24f, 54
Democratic-Republican party, 9, 11
DeWitt, Thomas, 110, 112
Dispensationalism, 120
Drake, Justice of New Jersey Court, 34
Dutch Reformed Church, 2, 21, 62, 68, 74, 85, chapter 11 passim
Dutch Reformed Seminary, 86

E

Edwards, Jonathan, 2
Everett, Edward, 30

F

Federalism, 24f, 27
Federalist party, 9, 11
Fillmore, Millard, 41
Finley, Robert, 1, 3-4, 8, 59-61, 68
First Great Awakening, 2
First Reformed Church of New Brunswick, 109, 112
Folsom, Joseph, 30, 63, 73
Force Bill, 16
Foster, Charles, 72
Fox, George, 32
Frelinghuysen, Ann, 1-3
Frelinghuysen, Eva, 2
Frelinghuysen, Frederick (brother), 1f, 107
Frelinghuysen, Frederick (father), 1-3, 9
Frelinghuysen, Frederick Theodore (nephew), 107-108, 113
Frelinghuysen, Gertrude, 1
Frelinghuysen, John, 1f
Frelinghuysen, Theodore J., x, 2, 4, 73

G

Garfield, President, 108
Garrison, William Lloyd, 20, 23, 61, 63-64
Griffin, Clifford, xiv, 72
Grundy, Felix, 79
Gurley, Ralph, 60

H

Hallock, William, 77
Hamilton, Alexander, 24-25
Hardenberg, Dinah, 1f, 85
Hardenberg, Jacobus, 3, 85
Harrison, William, 40, 42
Hatfield, Mark, 123
Hay, Dr., 110
Hayne, Robert, xiii

Henry, C.F., 83
Hertzog, Ann, 86
Hertzog, Peter, 86
Hertzog Theological Hall, 86, 91
Hicks, Elias, 29, 32f
Hicksites, 32f, 123-124
Hill, George William, 85
Howe, Daniel Walker, 47, 54, 72
Hunt, William, 41-42, 61

I

Ingersoll, Robert, 8

J

Jackson, Andrew, xiii, 11, 15f, 20f, 47, 51
Janeway, Edward, 85
Jay, John, 25
Jay, William, 64, 69
Jefferson, Thomas, x, 47, 51
Johnson, Richard, 19
Jordon, Barbara, 125

K

King, Thomas, 89
King, Martin Luther, 123, 125

L

Lewis, Tayler, 31, 87-88, 95, 106
Liberia, 60, 63, 67
Liberty party, 42-43
Lincoln, Abraham, x, 68-69, 82, 111
Lindsley, Philip, 8
Ludlow, John, 85

M

Madison, James, 3
Marshall, John, xiii, 59

Matthews, Donald, 72-73
Mayoralty of Newark (Frelinghuysen), 39f, 45
McIlvaine, Joseph, 11
Mercer, Charlotte, 106f
Monroe, James, 59
Moral Majority, 80
Morris Canal and Banking Company, 108

N

National-Republican party, 15, 17, 24, 29, 32, 34
Nevius, James S., 97f
New England Tract Society, 76
New Jersey Central Railroad, 108
New Jersey Colonization Society, 60
New Jersey Historical Society, 119
New Jersey Star Gazette (Trenton), 32
New York Times, 100
New York University, 44, 56, 75, 81f, 86-87, 90-91, 105, 118
Newark Daily Advertiser, 112
Nicaragua, 108
Nullification Crisis of 1832, 16

O

Old School-New School Presbyterianism, 48

P

Panic of 1837, xiv, 48, 71
Parker, Cortlandt, 7
Pennington, William, 96f, 101
Pension relief, 17, 27
Polk, James, 37, 42-43
Pompelly, Harriet, 107
Pre-millennialism, 79

Q

Quakers, 7, 32f, 35
Queen's College (Rutgers), 8

R

Randolph, John, 30, 59
Reagan, President, 123
Resolution of humiliation, fasting, and prayer, 18-19
Roosevelt, Franklin, x
Roosevelt, Teddy, x
Royko, Mike, 115
Rutgers College, 82, 84f, 91, 108f

S

Salt II Treaty, 118
Schlesinger, Arthur Jr., xv, 16, 49
Second Great Awakening, 47, 54, 73
Second Presbyterian Church (Newark), 4
Second Reformed Church of New Brunswick, 109, 113
Sentinel of Freedom (Newark), 112
Sergeant, John, 41
Sierra Leone, 60
Smith, J. Few, 112
Smith, Timothy, xv
Societies for Education and Aid to the Poor, 79f
Southard, Samuel, 8, 29, 32
Spring, Gardiner, 38
Staudenraus, P.J., 67
Stockton, Richard, 9
Strong, Theodore, 85
Sunday Call (Newark), 41
Sunday mail controversy, 19f, 27

T

Taney, Roger B., 24
Tappan, Arthur, 61
Tappan, Lewis, 37, 61
Tariff of 1833, 30
Taylor, William, J.R., 115
Tennent, Gilbert, 2
Treaty of Holston, 22
Turner, Nat, 63
Tyler, John, 40-41

U

University of Georgia, 60

V

Vice-presidential nomination of 1844 (Frelinghuysen), 40f, 99

W

Wall, Garret, 32, 34
War of 1812, 10, 18
Waring, Mrs. A.L., 104
Washington, George, x, 3, 23
Washington, Harold, ix
Webster, Daniel, xiii, 15, 30, 37, 44, 54, 59, 98
Whig party, xiv, 15, 29, 32, 39-40
Whiggery, 54f
Whitefield, George, 2
Wilberforce, William, x, xiii, 21, 60-61
Witherspoon, John, 4, 59-60
Wood, George, 32
Woodbridge, Dr. of Dutch Reformed Seminary, 105

About the Author

Dr. Robert J. Eells is Professor of History and Political Science at Trinity Christian College in Palos Heights, Illinois. He has also taught at Geneva College in Pennsylvania and Rockmont College in Colorado. He received his B.S. from Geneva College, his M.A. from Union College (Schenectady, New York), and the Ph.D. in American Studies from the University of New Mexico in Albuquerque. He is the author of over a dozen articles on Christianity and politics, as well as one previous book, *Lonely Walk: the Life of Senator Mark Hatfield*, published by Christian Herald Press in 1979. Dr. Eells lives in Oak Forest, Illinois with his wife, Janice, and son, Richard.